Preface

AF529328

It is a matter of great pleasure for us to present this book to our esteemed readers. This book has been designed as standard text on '(Advanced Cost Accounting & Cost System (Costs for Decision Making & Activity Based Costing (MM) (Course Code : 60110))' for M.Com.(Sem. - I)

This book comprehensively covers the entire syllabus of M.Com. Course of Savitribai Phule Pune University effective from June 2023 onwards. It has been written to meet the requirements of students of M.Com. Some of the special features of the book are as follows :

1. *Full coverage of the revised syllabus of M.Com.(Sem. - I)*
2. *Chapter outline at the beginning of each chapter to give a bird's eye view of the topics covered in the chapter.*
3. *Pointwise explanation of each topic in the chapter.*
4. *Topics are logically arranged in numbered paragraphs exactly according to the modified syllabus.*
5. *Proposed questions at the end of each chapter.*
6. *Extensive use of diagrams, tables and various forms to give visual view of key concepts and techniques.*
7. *Conversational, lucid and simple language.*

Every effort has been made to provide the readers with most up-to-date and authentic material on the subject.

We are very grateful to our publisher Mrs. and Mr. Rajesh Patne who have rendered all possible assistance in bringing out this book. We wish to acknowledge our deep gratitude to staff who have assisted and helped us in preparing this book. We will consider our efforts amply rewarded in case the book proves useful to the students and teachers of the subject.

Suggestions of readers are welcome and shall be acknowledged with gratitude.

With best wishes,

By Authors

Syllabus

M. Com. (Sem. - I) (MM) (Course Code : 60110)
Advanced Cost Accounting & Cost System
(Cost for Decision Making & Activity Based Costing)

Unit	Topic	No. of Lecture
1	**Costs for Decision Making** **1.** Revision of Cost concepts required for decision making (Marginal Cost, Differential or incremental Costs, Opportunity Cost, Out-of-Pocket Costs, Replacement Cost, Imputed Costs, Sunk Cost Committed Cost.) **2.** Meaning of 'Relevant and Irrelevant costs', Types of Relevant and Irrelevant Costs, Difference between Relevant and Irrelevant Costs, Decisions based on Relevant and Irrelevant Costs **3.** Make of Buy Decision **4.** Decision relating to 'Accepting or Rejecting an Order' **5.** Extra Shift Decision **6.** Decision relating to 'choosing best budget using only one limiting factor' **7.** Decision relating to 'adding or deleting departments or products' (Theory and Numerical Problems)	15
2	**Activity Based Costing** **1.** Meaning, Nature, and Scope of Activity Based Costing **2.** Difference between Traditional Costing and Activity Based Costing **3.** Meaning of terms used in Activity Based Costing – Activity, Cost Object, Cost Drivers, Cost Pool. **4.** Main Activities and its Cost Drivers **5.** Steps / Stages involved in Activity Based Costing / steps for calculating activity-based costing for a product **6.** Advantages of Activity Based Costing (Theory and Numerical Problems)	15

This Text Book is useful for Savitribai Phule Pune University and other Universities as well as Competitive Exams.

Advanced Cost Accounting & Cost System

(Costs for Decision Making & Activity Based Costing)

(MM) (Course Code : 60110)

M. Com. (Sem. - I)

Prin. Dr. Nitin L. Ghorpade
(M.Com., B.Ed., SET, M.Phil.,Ph.D)
Waghire college of Arts Commerce and Science, College,Saswad, Pune.

Dr. Shradha Prasad
(M.Com., M.Phil., SET., Ph.D)
Haribhai V. Desai College of Arts, Science and Commerce, Pune.

Dr. Deepa Nathwani
(M.Com., SET., Ph.D.)
Manghanmal Udharam College of Commerce, Pune.

Dr. Kishor H. Kaldante
(M.Com., G.D.C &A.,M.Phil., NET., SET., DSM., Ph.D)
Annasaheb Waghire Arts, Commerce and Science College, Otur, Pune.

2023

Price. 110/-

SUCCESS PUBLICATIONS

Published by
Dr. Rajesh M. Patne
Success Publications
Radha Krishna Apartment, 535, Shaniwar Peth,
Appa Balwant Chowk, Opp. Prabhat Talkies, Pune - 411 030.
Ph. 24434662 Mobile : 9325315464.

Edition
2023

Edited By
Miss. Rajashree Patne

Typesetting, Layout
Miss. Varsha Lokhande

Cover Designing
Miss. Pooja Deshpande

ISBN NO. - 978-81-19180-45-5

INDEX

M. Com. (Sem. - I) (MM) (Course Code : 60110)
Advanced Cost Accounting & Cost System
(Cost for Decision Making & Activity Based Costing)

UNIT 1

Cost for Decision Making

- 1.1 Revision of Cost Concepts Required for Decision Making
- 1.2 Relevant and Irrelevant Costs
- 1.3 Make of Buy Decision
- 1.4 Decision Relating to 'Accepting or Rejecting an Order'
- 1.5 Extra Shirt Decision
- 1.6 Decision Relating to 'Choosing best budget using only one limiting factor'
- 1.7 Decision Relating to 'Adding or Deleting Departments or Products'

Introduction :

Cost is a pivotal consideration in decision-making because it directly influences the feasibility, profitability, and sustainability of any endeavor. From personal choices such as purchasing a car to organizational decisions like launching a new product, understanding and effectively managing costs is essential for making informed and rational choices.

This introduction explores the significance of cost in decision-making, highlighting how it factors into various scenarios and its impact on outcomes. We will delve into the various types of costs, the methods used to analyze them, and how businesses and individuals can navigate the intricate landscape of costs to make sound decisions. Whether minimizing costs to maximize profits, evaluating trade-offs, or assessing the long-term implications of choices, the role of cost in decision-making is undeniable

1.1 Revision of Cost Concepts Required for Decision Making :

1.1.1 Concept of Marginal cost for decision making:

Marginal cost is a fundamental concept in economics and decision-making. It represents the additional cost incurred when producing one more unit of a good or service. Marginal cost is crucial for making short-term business decisions, especially when determining optimal production levels and pricing strategies. Here's a closer look at the concept of marginal cost and its significance in decision-making:

A) Definition of Marginal Cost:

Marginal cost (MC) is calculated by dividing the change in total cost by the change in quantity produced. In mathematical terms:

B) Key Points about Marginal Cost:

Key Points about Marginal Costs are as follows :

1) Incremental Cost:

Marginal cost focuses on the cost of producing one additional unit of output. It reflects the cost increase when production is increased by one unit.

2) Variable Costs:

Marginal cost primarily considers variable costs, which change with the level of production. Fixed costs, such as rent and salaries, are not included in the calculation.

3) Law of Diminishing Returns:

As production increases, marginal cost may rise due to diminishing marginal returns. This means that at some point, producing additional units leads to less efficient use of resources and increased costs.

C) Significance in Decision-Making:

Marginal cost is a critical tool for making various short-term decisions in business:

1) Production Level:

Businesses can use marginal cost to determine the optimal production level. It helps find the quantity at which marginal cost equals marginal revenue, resulting in maximum profit.

2) Pricing Strategy:

When setting prices for products or services, understanding marginal cost is essential. Prices should ideally cover at least the marginal cost to ensure each sale contributes positively to covering variable expenses.

3) Special Orders:

When faced with special orders or bulk purchase requests, businesses can evaluate whether accepting the order would cover the additional marginal cost and contribute to profit.

4) Make or Buy Decisions:

For manufacturers, marginal cost can assist in deciding whether to produce a component in-house or purchase it externally. If the marginal cost of producing the component exceeds the purchase cost, outsourcing might be more cost-effective.

5) Inventory Management:

Businesses can use marginal cost to determine whether it's economically feasible to produce more units and increase inventory levels.

6) Resource Allocation:

In cases where resources are limited, marginal cost helps allocate resources efficiently. Resources are directed to activities where the marginal benefit exceeds the marginal cost.

7) Short-Term Planning:

Marginal cost aids in short-term planning by providing insights into cost variations as production levels change.

D) Limitations:

While marginal cost is valuable for short-term decisions, it does have limitations:

1) It assumes that fixed costs remain constant, which might not hold true in the long run.
2) It doesn't consider the impact of decisions on long-term profitability or strategic goals.
3) It assumes that all units produced are identical and doesn't account for variations in product quality or customer preferences.

In conclusion, marginal cost is a pivotal concept for making short-term operational decisions. It guides businesses in optimizing production levels, pricing strategies, and resource allocation to maximize profitability.

1.1.2 Differential or Incremental costs for decision making :

Differential costs, also known as incremental costs, play a crucial role in decision-making for businesses and organizations. These costs represent the difference in total costs between two alternative courses of action, helping decision-makers evaluate the financial impact of various choices.

A) Definition of Differential Costs:

Differential costs are the additional costs that arise from choosing one alternative over another. They involve comparing the costs associated with different options or scenarios. Differential costs can include both variable and fixed costs that change due to the decision being considered.

B) Key Points about Differential Costs:

Key Points about Differential Costs are as follows :

1) Comparison Basis:

Differential costs are determined by comparing the costs of one decision option to those of another. These comparisons are essential for evaluating the financial implications of different choices.

2) Incremental Perspective:

Differential costs focus on the incremental changes in costs resulting from a particular decision. They help quantify the impact of a decision on costs compared to the current situation.

3) Avoidable Costs:

Differential costs often consist of avoidable costs – costs that can be eliminated or reduced if a particular alternative is chosen. These costs directly influence the decision's financial impact.

C) Significance in Decision-Making:

Differential costs are critical for making various types of decisions within an organization:

1) Make or Buy Decisions:

Businesses assess whether to produce a component in-house or purchase it externally. The differential cost is the difference between producing the item internally versus buying it externally.

2) Accept or Reject Special Orders:

When faced with special orders or bulk purchase requests, organizations evaluate whether the incremental revenue from accepting the order exceeds the incremental costs.

3) Equipment Replacement:

When deciding whether to replace old equipment with new equipment, differential costs help compare the costs of maintaining the old equipment versus the costs of purchasing and operating the new equipment.

4) Product Line Decisions:

Companies analyze the costs and revenues associated with different product lines to determine which lines are contributing positively to profit.

5) Adding or Dropping Product Lines:

Differential costs assist in evaluating the financial impact of introducing new product lines or discontinuing existing ones.

6) Investment Projects:

For capital investment decisions, differential costs help assess whether the incremental cash flows generated by the investment exceed the incremental costs.

7) Shut Down Decisions:

In situations where a segment of a business is not performing well, organizations compare the costs of continuing the operation to the costs of shutting it down.

D) Limitations:

While differential costs are valuable decision-making tools, they have some limitations:

1) They focus solely on financial aspects and may not consider non-financial factors like quality, customer satisfaction, and long-term strategic goals.
2) The determination of relevant differential costs can sometimes be complex, particularly

when indirect costs and opportunity costs are involved.

In conclusion, differential costs provide decision-makers with a quantitative assessment of the financial impact of choosing one option over another.

1.1.3 Opportunity Cost for Decision Making :

Opportunity cost is a fundamental concept in economics and decision-making that refers to the value of the next best alternative foregone when a choice is made. It represents the benefits or potential gains that could have been obtained by choosing an alternative course of action instead of the one that was chosen. Understanding opportunity cost is crucial for making rational decisions, evaluating trade-offs, and allocating resources effectively.

A) Definition of Opportunity Cost:

Opportunity cost is the value of the benefits or returns that could have been gained from choosing an alternative option, but were not chosen due to the decision made. It's the "cost" of not pursuing the next best alternative.

B) Key Points about Opportunity Cost:

Key Points about Opportunity Cost are as follows :

1) Relative Comparison:

Opportunity cost involves comparing the benefits of one decision to the benefits of the best alternative. It considers the relative value of alternatives in terms of their potential outcomes.

2) Implicit Cost:

Opportunity cost is often implicit and not explicitly measured in monetary terms. It encompasses both tangible and intangible benefits that could have been gained from choosing an alternative action.

3) Time Dependency:

Opportunity cost is closely linked to the concept of time. The longer an option is pursued, the greater the opportunity cost associated with not choosing an alternative with potentially higher returns.

C) Significance in Decision-Making:

Opportunity cost plays a pivotal role in various types of decisions:

1) Resource Allocation:

Businesses allocate their limited resources (time, money, labor) to different projects or activities. The opportunity cost of choosing one project over another is the potential benefit lost from not choosing the alternative project.

2) Investment Choices:

When deciding between investment opportunities, understanding opportunity cost helps evaluate the potential returns that could be achieved by investing in other opportunities.

3) Time Management:

Individuals allocate their time among various activities. The opportunity cost of spending time on one task is the potential benefit lost from not spending that time on a more valuable activity.

4) Education and Career Decisions:

Individuals decide whether to pursue education, training, or employment opportunities. The opportunity cost is the potential earnings that could have been gained from an alternative choice.

5) Productivity and Efficiency:

In business operations, understanding opportunity cost helps identify which tasks or processes contribute the most value and should be prioritized.

D) Example of Opportunity Cost:

Imagine you have two investment options: Option A offers a guaranteed return of 5% annually, while Option B is riskier but has the potential to yield a higher return of 8%. If you choose Option A, the opportunity cost is the potential additional 3% return that you could have earned from Option B.

E) Limitations:

While opportunity cost is a valuable concept, it has some limitations:

1) It may be challenging to quantify the exact value of opportunity cost, especially for intangible benefits.
2) Decisions involving opportunity cost assume that benefits and costs are known with certainty, which may not always be the case.

In conclusion, opportunity cost highlights the trade-offs and choices individuals and organizations face when making decisions.

1.1.4 Out of Pocket Costs for Decision Making :

Out-of-pocket costs, also known as explicit costs, are the direct and measurable expenses that a business or individual incurs when making a specific decision. These costs involve actual cash payments or expenditures for resources and services. Understanding out-of-pocket costs is essential for accurate financial analysis, budgeting, and decision-making. Let's explore the concept of out-of-pocket costs and their significance in decision-making:

A) Definition of Out-of-Pocket Costs:

Out-of-pocket costs are the explicit monetary expenses that result from a particular decision. These costs can be easily identified and measured as they involve actual cash payments or financial transactions.

B) Key Points about Out-of-Pocket Costs:

Key Points about Out-of-Pocket Costs are as follows :

1) **Tangible Expenses:**

   Out-of-pocket costs are tangible and measurable expenses that appear on a company's financial statements or personal budget.

2) **Direct Relation:**

   These costs are directly related to the decision being made and are incurred as a direct consequence of that decision.

3) **Short-Term Focus:**

   Out-of-pocket costs are primarily short-term costs that affect the immediate financial position of a business or individual.

C) Significance in Decision-Making:

Out-of-pocket costs are crucial for making a variety of business and personal decisions:

1) **Cost Control:**

   Organizations track out-of-pocket costs to manage expenses and ensure that they stay within budgeted limits.

2) **Investment Decisions:**

   When evaluating investment opportunities, out-of-pocket costs help assess the immediate cash outflows required to initiate the investment.

3) **Purchasing Decisions:**

   Consumers and businesses consider out-of-pocket costs when purchasing goods and services, comparing prices and benefits.

4) **Project Evaluation:**

   Businesses assess the out-of-pocket costs associated with a project, including initial setup, ongoing expenses, and potential returns.

5) **Marketing and Advertising:**

   Businesses analyze out-of-pocket costs related to advertising campaigns, events, and promotional activities.

6) **Capital Expenditures:**

   When deciding on major capital expenditures, organizations evaluate the out-of-pocket costs of purchasing, operating, and maintaining the asset.

D) Example of Out-of-Pocket Costs:

Imagine a company considering the purchase of a new piece of equipment. The out-of-pocket costs would include the purchase price of the equipment, installation costs, any associated taxes, and fees.

E) Limitations:

While out-of-pocket costs are valuable for decision-making, they have limitations:

1) They focus solely on the explicit monetary expenses and may not capture hidden or indirect costs.

2) Long-term implications and non-financial factors may not be fully considered when focusing solely on out-of-pocket costs.

In conclusion, out-of-pocket costs provide a clear understanding of the immediate financial impact of a decision.

1.1.5 Replacement Costs :

Replacement cost is a concept used in decision-making, particularly in situations involving asset management, equipment maintenance, and capital expenditure choices. It refers to the cost of replacing an asset or item with an identical or similar one at its current market price. Understanding replacement costs is essential for evaluating whether it's more cost-effective to repair, maintain, or replace an asset. Let's explore the concept of replacement costs and their significance in decision-making:

A) Definition of Replacement Cost:

Replacement cost is the expense associated with acquiring a new asset or item to replace an existing one. It reflects the current market value of the asset being replaced and considers factors such as purchase price, transportation, installation, and any associated costs.

B) Key Points about Replacement Costs:

Key Points about Replacement Costs are as follows :

1) Current Market Value:

Replacement cost considers the price of obtaining a new asset that is equivalent to the one being replaced, taking into account any changes in market conditions or technology.

2) Comparable Replacement:

The replacement cost is based on the cost of acquiring an asset that has similar features, specifications, and functionalities to the existing asset.

3) Capital Expenditure Decisions:

Replacement costs are crucial in deciding whether to repair, maintain, or replace assets, especially in cases where assets have reached the end of their useful life or become obsolete.

C) Significance in Decision-Making:

Replacement costs play a significant role in various decision-making scenarios:

1) Asset Maintenance vs. Replacement:

Organizations compare the costs of maintaining an aging or faulty asset with the cost of replacing it with a newer, more efficient asset.

2) Capital Budgeting:

When evaluating capital expenditure projects, businesses assess whether investing in new equipment or technology is more cost-effective than continuing to use the existing assets.

3) **Insurance Claims:**

In cases of asset loss or damage, insurance companies consider the replacement cost to determine the appropriate compensation amount.

4) **Depreciation and Asset Valuation:**

Replacement cost is used to estimate the current value of assets for financial reporting purposes, including determining depreciation and asset impairment.

5) **Inventory Management:**

Organizations consider replacement costs when deciding whether to restock inventory items or discontinue products.

D) **Example of Replacement Cost:**

Consider a manufacturing company that owns a piece of machinery used in production. If the machinery breaks down and cannot be repaired economically, the company must decide whether to replace it. The replacement cost would include the purchase price of a similar or equivalent machine, delivery and installation costs, and any additional expenses required to get the new machine operational.

E) **Limitations:**

While replacement costs are valuable for decision-making, they have limitations:

1) They focus on monetary considerations and may not fully account for non-financial factors like potential operational disruptions or impacts on production efficiency.
2) Replacement costs assume that a suitable replacement is readily available, which might not always be the case for specialized or custom equipment.

In conclusion, replacement costs provide insights into the financial impact of replacing assets or items in various decision-making contexts.

1.1.6 Imputed Costs :

Imputed costs are hypothetical or notional costs that are not incurred in actual monetary transactions but are assigned to various resources or activities for decision-making and accounting purposes. These costs represent the value of resources that are used within an organization but for which no external monetary payment is made. Imputed costs are used to reflect the economic reality of resource usage, even if no explicit cash transactions occur. They are particularly relevant in scenarios where resources are used internally, and their opportunity cost needs to be considered. Let's explore the concept of imputed costs and their significance in decision-making:

A) **Key Points about Imputed Costs:**

Key Points about Imputed Costs are as follows :

1) **Hypothetical Nature:**

Imputed costs are not actual expenses incurred; instead, they are estimated costs assigned for analytical and decision-making purposes.

2) Opportunity Cost:

Imputed costs reflect the opportunity cost of using internal resources, which could have been used elsewhere to generate value.

3) Accounting and Reporting:

Imputed costs are used for internal accounting and reporting to provide a more accurate representation of resource usage and economic performance.

B) Significance in Decision-Making:

Imputed costs are used to address several decision-making scenarios:

1) Lease vs. Buy Decisions:

In decisions involving leasing or owning assets, imputed costs help compare the financial implications of different options.

2) Internal Resource Allocation:

Imputed costs aid in allocating shared resources and facilities costs to different departments or projects within an organization.

3) Cost-Benefit Analysis:

When assessing projects or investments that utilize internal resources, imputed costs are considered to accurately assess the benefits and costs.

4) Government and Public Policy:

Imputed costs are used in public policy discussions to account for the value of non-market activities or benefits.

C) Example of Imputed Cost:

Consider a company that owns its office building. Instead of renting the space to another tenant and generating rental income, the company uses the space for its own operations. In this scenario, an imputed rental cost is assigned to the company's operations to account for the opportunity cost of not generating rental income from the space.

D) Limitations:

Imputed costs have some limitations to consider:

1) They are based on estimates and assumptions, which might introduce subjectivity and variability into decision-making.
2) The imputation process can be complex and may require careful analysis and consideration of various factors.

In conclusion, imputed costs are valuable tools for decision-making, allowing organizations to account for the opportunity costs of using internal resources and facilities.

1.1.7 Sunk Cost :

Sunk costs are costs that have already been incurred and cannot be recovered, regardless of the decision made. These costs are irrelevant to future decision-making because they are spent and cannot be changed or recovered. Understanding sunk costs is essential for making rational and forward-looking decisions, as they should not influence choices about future actions. Let's delve into the concept of sunk costs and their significance in decision-making:

A) Key Points about Sunk Cost:

Key Points about Sunk Cost are as follows :

1) Irrecoverable:

Sunk costs are costs that have been expended and cannot be recovered, regardless of the future course of action.

2) Past Expenses:

Sunk costs represent expenditures made in the past, and they should not be factored into decisions about future actions.

3) Irrelevance:

Sunk costs are irrelevant to decision-making because they cannot be changed or influenced by the current or future decisions.

B) Significance in Decision-Making:

The primary significance of understanding sunk costs lies in avoiding their undue influence on decision-making:

1) Project Abandonment:

When evaluating whether to continue or abandon a project, sunk costs should not be considered. Only future costs and benefits matter.

2) Investment Decisions:

Sunk costs should not be a factor when assessing the financial viability of an investment or opportunity.

3) Resource Allocation:

Sunk costs should not be a factor when allocating resources or making choices between different options.

C) Example of Sunk Costs:

Consider a company that has invested a substantial amount of money in developing a new software product. If the software project is not progressing well and there are doubts about its potential success, the money already spent on development is a sunk cost. The decision to continue or abandon the project should be based on the project's current and future potential, not on the sunk costs.

D) Limitations:

Despite understanding the concept of sunk costs, individuals and organizations can still fall victim to the "sunk cost fallacy," where they continue investing resources into a failing project or endeavor because they've already invested so much. This fallacy stems from emotional attachment to past investments.

In conclusion, recognizing and disregarding sunk costs is a fundamental aspect of rational decision-making.

1.1.8 Committed Cost for Decision Making :

Committed costs, also known as fixed costs or contractual costs, are expenses that a business or individual is obligated to pay due to contractual agreements, legal commitments, or long-term arrangements. These costs are not influenced by short-term decisions and remain constant regardless of the level of business activity or production. Understanding committed costs is important for budgeting, financial planning, and evaluating the impact of short-term decisions on long-term obligations.

A) Key Points about Committed Costs :

Key Points about Committed Costs are as follows :

1) Obligatory Expenses:

Committed costs are expenses that must be paid due to existing contractual or legal obligations. They often include items like rent, lease payments, insurance premiums, and loan interest.

2) Fixed Nature:

Committed costs remain constant over a specified period, such as a month or a year, regardless of changes in production levels or business activities.

3) Long-Term Perspective:

Committed costs are typically associated with long-term agreements and arrangements, and they continue regardless of short-term decisions.

B) Significance in Decision-Making:

While committed costs are not influenced by short-term decisions, understanding them is essential for effective decision-making:

1) Budgeting and Financial Planning:

Committed costs provide a baseline for budgeting and financial forecasting, allowing businesses to allocate resources and plan for future expenses.

2) Cost-Volume-Profit Analysis:

Committed costs are considered when conducting cost-volume-profit (CVP) analysis, helping to determine the breakeven point and assess profitability.

3) Investment and Expansion Decisions:

When evaluating investment opportunities or expansion plans, committed costs are factored in to assess the overall financial feasibility of the decision.

4) Contract Renewal or Termination:

Committed costs play a role in evaluating whether to renew or terminate long-term contracts, such as leases or service agreements.

C) Example of Committed Cost:

Consider a company that has a lease agreement for office space. The monthly rent is a committed cost because it remains the same regardless of the company's production levels or business activities. Even if the company's output decreases or increases, the rent expense remains a constant obligation.

D) Limitations:

Committed costs have limitations to consider:

1) While committed costs are consistent over a specified period, some contracts or agreements might allow for negotiation or adjustment under specific circumstances.
2) Focusing solely on committed costs might lead to overlooking variable costs and other factors that influence decision-making.

In conclusion, committed costs are important components of financial planning and decision-making.

1.2 Relevant and Irrelevant Costs :

In the short term decision making the management will consider the relevant cost of the cost element and irrelevant cost of the cost element. for decision making purpose cost can be classified into : 1) Relevant Cost, 2) Irrelevant Cost.

1.2.1 Meaning & Definition of Relevant and Irrelevant costs :

A) Meaning of Relevant costs :

Relevant costs refer to expenses that have a direct impact on a specific decision or choice. These costs are future-oriented and have the potential to change based on the different alternatives being considered. Relevant costs are crucial in decision-making because they help assess the financial implications of different options and guide individuals and businesses towards making the most economically advantageous choices.

When analyzing relevant costs, it's important to focus on expenses that are directly affected by the decision at hand. Irrelevant costs, such as sunk costs (expenses that have already been incurred and cannot be recovered) or costs that won't change regardless of the decision, should be excluded from the analysis.

B) Definition of Relevant costs :

Definition of Relevant costs are as follows :

1) **Peter Drucker:**

   "Future costs that differ among alternative courses of action."

2) **Horngren, Foster, and Datar:**

   "Costs that will be affected by a decision. They are costs that differ among alternatives."

3) **Robert S. Kaplan:**

   "Costs that will be changed—or incurred—if a particular alternative course of action is selected."

C) Meaning Irrelevant costs :

Irrelevant costs are expenses that do not directly affect or influence a specific decision or choice. These costs are not impacted by the various alternatives being considered and therefore do not play a role in guiding decision-making. Irrelevant costs are typically expenses that have already been incurred and cannot be changed, or costs that remain constant regardless of the decision taken.

When evaluating different options, it's important to focus on relevant costs, which are expenses that vary based on the alternatives being considered and directly impact the decision's financial outcome. Ignoring irrelevant costs is essential for making rational and economically sound choices, as including them in the analysis can lead to distorted conclusions and influence decisions based on factors that do not contribute to the decision's outcome.

D) Definition Irrelevant costs :

Definition Irrelevant costs are as follows :

1) Horngren, Foster, and Datar:

"Costs that do not differ among alternatives being considered. These costs will be the same regardless of which alternative is chosen."

2) Thomas L. Albright:

"Those costs that will not be changed regardless of the alternative selected."

3) Colin Drury:

"Costs that will remain unaffected by a specific managerial decision."

1.2.2 Types of Relevant and Irrelevant Costs :

A) Types of Relevant Costs :

Types of Relevant Costs are as follows :

1) Incremental Costs :

Incremental costs are expenses that change as a direct result of a specific decision. They are relevant because they provide insight into the additional expenses incurred due to the decision. For example, when a company decides to produce more units of a product, the additional costs of raw materials, labor, and production overhead are incremental costs.

2) Opportunity Costs :

Opportunity costs represent the value of the next best alternative forgone when a decision is made. While not a monetary expense, opportunity costs are crucial in decision-making because they reflect what could have been gained by choosing a different option. For instance, if a company decides to allocate resources to Project A instead of Project B, the potential gains from Project B become the opportunity cost of choosing Project A.

3) Marginal Costs :

Marginal costs refer to the cost of producing one additional unit of a product or service. They are relevant in decisions where the goal is to maximize profit by analyzing whether the incremental revenue from producing one more unit exceeds the additional cost.

4) Avoidable Costs :

Avoidable costs are expenses that can be eliminated or reduced by choosing a particular alternative. These costs are directly impacted by the decision and therefore relevant. In outsourcing decisions, the avoidable costs might include expenses associated with producing in-house that can be avoided by outsourcing.

B) Types of Irrelevant Costs :

Types of Irrelevant Costs are as follows :

1) Sunk Costs :

Sunk costs are expenses that have already been incurred and cannot be recovered. They are irrelevant because they are unrecoverable and should not influence future decisions. For example, the money spent on research and development for a project that was ultimately abandoned is a sunk cost.

2) Fixed Costs :

Fixed costs remain constant regardless of the decision being made. Since they don't change with different alternatives, they are often considered irrelevant in short-term decision-making. For instance, when deciding to accept a special order, fixed manufacturing overhead costs might be considered irrelevant.

3) Committed Costs :

Committed costs are expenses that an organization is obligated to pay due to prior contractual agreements or ongoing commitments. These costs are predetermined and unchangeable, making them irrelevant when making decisions involving alternative choices.

4) Past Costs :

Costs incurred in the past, regardless of their amount, are irrelevant for future decisions. Only future costs and potential benefits should be considered when evaluating alternatives.

5) Indirect Costs :

Indirect costs, also known as overhead costs, are expenses that cannot be directly traced to a specific product or project. While they are relevant in calculating the overall cost structure, they might be considered irrelevant in specific decisions where the focus is on direct costs.

1.2.3 Difference between Relevant and Irrelevant Costs :

Difference between Relevant and Irrelevant Costs are as follows :

Point	Relevant Costs	Irrelevant Cost
1) Definition	Costs that influence decision-making and outcomes	Costs that do not impact decision-making or outcomes.
2) Consideration	Considered when making decisions	Not considered when making decisions
3) Impact	Affects the choice between alternatives	Does not impact the choice between alternatives
4) Future oriented	Future costs that will change based on decisions.	Historical or sunk costs that cannot be changed.
5) Examples	Direct materials costs for producing a product - Additional labor costs for a new project	Past advertising costs. - Sunk research and development expenses.
6) Decision making	Included in analyzing options to make informed choices.	Excluded from the decision-making process
7) Relevance	Depends on the specific decision being made	Generally not tied to specific decisions

1.2.4 Decision based on Relevant and Irrelevant Costs :

In the intricate realm of organizational management, decisions serve as the linchpin that shapes the trajectory of success. The discernment to make well-informed choices is the hallmark of effective leadership, impacting an organization's efficiency, profitability, and long-term sustainability. Within the framework of decision-making, the interplay between relevant and irrelevant costs emerges as a pivotal dimension.

1) **Decoding Relevance:**

   Relevant costs stand as the compass that guides the decision-making process. They encompass costs that are directly impacted by a specific decision, rendering them pivotal in shaping the alternatives under consideration. Irrelevant costs, on the other hand, remain impervious to the decision at hand, holding no bearing on the course of action. The ability to distinguish between these two cost categories is instrumental in maintaining decision-making precision.

2) **Strategic Cost Classification:**

   Embedded within the strategic fabric of an organization, the distinction between relevant and irrelevant costs shapes the contours of decision relevance. Relevant costs, as the financial focal points, direct attention to the variables that tangibly influence outcomes. In contrast, irrelevant costs, when permitted to enter the decision arena, can introduce distortions that cloud judgment. The strategic classification of costs engenders clarity by isolating cost elements that wield influence from those that are inconsequential.

3) **Make or Buy Dilemma:**

The quandary of deciding whether to produce an essential component in-house or procure it externally encapsulates the essence of cost relevance. For this decision, relevant costs encompass production expenses that experience alteration based on the chosen path. These comprise direct materials, labor, and variable overhead. Meanwhile, irrelevant costs, including past expenditures or fixed overhead, hold no sway in steering the decision, underpinning the rationale behind their exclusion.

4) **Special Order Assessment:**

When confronted with a unique order that deviates from customary pricing, assessing its viability entails a scrutiny of both relevant and irrelevant costs. Relevant costs, here, encompass the incremental expenses linked directly to fulfilling the special order. This includes supplementary raw materials, labor, and overhead. Contrarily, irrelevant costs pertain to regular production costs that are unaffected by the deviation from the norm.

5) **Product Line Evaluation:**

Determining whether to persist with or discontinue a particular product line mandates a comprehensive evaluation. Within this evaluation, relevant costs materialize as the linchpin. They encompass costs tied exclusively to the specific product line, such as direct materials, labor, and variable overhead. Irrelevant costs, constituting fixed overhead that stands impervious to the product line's continuation or cessation, find no foothold in the decision-making process.

6) **Equipment Replacement Strategy:**

The intricate decision of replacing outdated equipment with modern counterparts hinges on an appreciation of cost relevance. Pertinent costs encompass the spectrum of new equipment, installation expenses, and potential disposals of the antiquated machinery. Irrelevant costs, encapsulating historical expenditures tethered to the old equipment, are detached from the decision's gravitational pull.

7) **Holistic Decision-Making Process:**

The assimilation of both relevant and irrelevant costs unfurls as a strategic choreography. The initial step involves a meticulous identification of costs that metamorphose in accordance with the decision. These relevant costs become the bedrock of decision-making, rendering it insightful and actionable. Simultaneously, irrelevant costs are pruned away, shielding the decision-making process from distortions.

8) Mitigating Cognitive Biases:

The exclusion of irrelevant costs resonates as a cognitive safeguard against the sunk cost fallacy. This fallacy, which entraps decision-makers in past investments, is dismantled as irrelevant costs are sidelined. This enables decision-makers to retain focus on the path ahead without the encumbrance of past expenditures.

9) Evaluating Long-Term Sustainability:

The compass of relevance guides organizations towards decisions that align harmoniously with long-term goals. By encapsulating the long-term impact of decisions, organizations ensure alignment with strategic objectives, fostering a dynamic harmony between short-term actions and long-term vision.

10) Resource Allocation Paragon:

Relevant costs metamorphose into an instrument of precision in resource allocation. By honing in on costs that shape outcomes, organizations orchestrate resource allocation that optimizes efficiency and maximizes profitability. Excluding irrelevant costs safeguards against skewed allocations that can compromise profitability.

11) Educating Decision-Makers:

The cognizance of relevant and irrelevant costs permeates the organizational echelons, equipping decision-makers at every level with a discerning lens. This institutional awareness culminates in more prudent and calculated decisions, fostering alignment with overarching strategies.

12) Championing Informed Choices:

The amalgamation of relevant and irrelevant costs cultivates an environment of astute decision-making. This amalgamation acts as a beacon, illuminating the path toward choices that resonate with strategic imperatives, fortifying organizations against the winds of uncertainty.

Conclusion:

Within the intricate fabric of decision-making, the synergy between relevant and irrelevant costs assumes paramount importance. The integration of these cost categories is akin to an intricate dance, harmonizing the financial landscape and ensuring that decisions are based on sound financial judgment. Organizations that adeptly discern the relevance of costs, while meticulously excluding the irrelevant, stand poised to navigate the labyrinth of decisions with poise and precision.

1.3 Make or Buy Decision :

Very often management is confronted with the problem of deciding whether to buy a component or product from an outside source or to manufacture the same if it is economical as compared to the price quoted by a supplier. In deciding the absorption costing would mislead. If the decision is to buy from an external source the price quoted by the supplier should be less than marginal cost. If the decision is to make within the organisation, the cost of production should include all additional cost such as depreciation on new plant interest on capita, etc. If this cost of production is less than the quotation price, it should be decided making the product rather than procure it from an external source.

A) Meaning :

Make-or-Buy decision (also called the outsourcing decision) is a judgment made by management whether to make a component internally or buy it from the market. While making the decision, both qualitative and quantitative factors must be considered. Examples of the qualitative factors in make-or-buy decision are: control over quality of the component, reliability of suppliers, and impact of the decision on suppliers and customers, etc. The quantitative factors are actually the incremental costs resulting from making or buying the component. For example: incremental production cost per unit, purchase cost per unit, production capacity available to manufacture the component, etc.

B) Factors Influencing on Make or Buy Decision :

In a make or buy decision the following cost and non-cost factors must be considered specifically.

1) Cost Factors :

i) Availability of plant facility.

ii) Quality and type of item which affects the production schedule

iii) The space required for the production of item.

iv) Any special machinery or equipment required.

v) Any transportation involved due to the location of production

vi) Cost of acquiring special know how required for the item.

2) Replacing Existing Machinery with New Machinery :

Sometimes with a view to derive maximum efficiency an existing plant may have to be replaced by a new one. Again the guiding factors mentioned earlier will help in such decision making process.

a) Items of Differential Costs :

i) Capital equipment and associated costs, viz., interest, depreciation, etc.,

ii) Loss on sale of old equipment

iii) Increased in fixed overhead costs.

b) Items of Differential Benefits :

i) Saving in operating costs.

ii) Increased volume and value of production

iii) Realizable value of old machine

iv) Tax benefits, if any.

3) Alternative Use of Plant or Productive Facility :

To take advantage of alternative use of production facility or alternative use of plant it is necessary to know the contribution margin. That alternative which yields highest contribution margin shall be selected.

4) Product Mix, Profit Planning and Profit Maximization :

Companies manufacturing varieties of products often have to decide which product mi8xc is more profitable. That product mix which gives maximum contribution is to be considered as best product mixes. Similarly, profit planning is often considered so as to earn reasonable profit if not maximum profit. The profit planning is affected by factors such as i) volume of output, ii) Product mix, iii) costs to be incurred, iv) Prices to be charged and so on. Marginal costing techniques guide the management in this regard.

5) Avoidable and Unavoidable Cost :

Avoidable costs are those which can be eliminated if a particular product or department, with which they are directly related, is discontinued. Unavoidable cost is that cost which will not be eliminated with the discontinuation of a product or department.

6) Relevant Cost and Irrelevant Cost :

A cost that is relevant to a decision is called relevant cost. Past costs are not generally relevant costs because they are sunk costs or costs already incurred. Thus the book value of an asset or depreciation charged in accounts in respect of an asset is not relevant cost. On the other hand, the fall in the resale value of an asset as a result of using it, as also the running expenses incurred to make use of the asset are relevant costs.

7) Profitability of the Department or Products:

The preparation of a departmental profit and loss account under marginal costing is useful in determining which department is making profit and which department is incurring a loss. This enables the management to decide whether a particular department, must continue operation or it should be eliminated. The decision is taken by referring to the contribution made or loss incurred by the department or product.

C) Functional Aspects of Make or Buy Decision:

Make or buy decision should be viewed with both long term and short term perspectives i11 mind. Some of the effects are tangible and others are intangible. These are classified as follows:

1) Financial Aspects:

The make decision is always demands an investment in plant, machineries and equipment. The investments can be categorized in to fixed cost and variable cost. The buy decision is associated with only variable cost. Expressing all factors in to money terms carries out a thorough and comparative analysis. Then the decision is to be taken based on which one is more economical to make or to buy.

2) Technological Aspects :

The make or buy decision is influenced by

a) The access to the latest technology to the organisation.

b) Feasibility and terms and conditions of technology transfer.

c) Outdating of technology.

d) Product life cycle.

3) Marketing Aspects:

The marketing aspects have the influence on make or buy decision. When there is a fierce competition, an organisation tries to enhance the quality and cut down the costs. The make decision assures the quality and reliability of the parts. Under the situation of increasing market share and a good future sales potential company can have an additional investment potential and hence can opt for make decision. When there is a doubt about the market potential, the company should opt for buy decision. The large organisations pay greater attention to quality which favors the make decision to maintain quality and reliability of items.

4) Purchasing Aspects :

The decision is influenced by:

a) The availability of items or components in sufficient quantities.

b) The delivery commitments must be reliably met.

c) The acceptable quality and price level of the product.

d) Economy in transportation from the source to the organisation.

e) Competence and reliability of vendors.

5) Strategic Aspects :

Any decision that is to be taken including make or buy decision should be taken with due consideration to overall objective of the organisation. Due importance should be given to the economy, secrecy and flexibility in taking decision regarding make or buy.

6) Intangible Aspects :

Intangible aspects like environmental factors, labour union acceptance, goodwill, support to ancilliariasation and growth of SSI units, technical assistance to vendors also influences the make or buy decision.

D) Economic and non-economic Factors Influencing Make or Buy Decisions :

Decisions regarding whether to make or buy the components involve both economic and non-economic factors. Economically, an item or component is a candidate for in house production, if the company has sufficient capacity and if the components value is high enough to cover the variable costs of production and make some contribution towards the fixed cost. Low volumes favor buying, which incurs very little or no fixed costs. Following Fig. shows the relationship between cost factors. The non-economic factors are :

1) Availability of Infrastructure and Skilled Personnel.
2) Desire for Alternate Sources of Supply.
3) Employee Preferences and Stability Concern.
4) Need to Maintain Trade Secrets.
5) Desire to Expand in to New Product Line.
6) Forward or backward integration.
7) Long Lasting and Mutually Rewarding Relationships with Vendors.

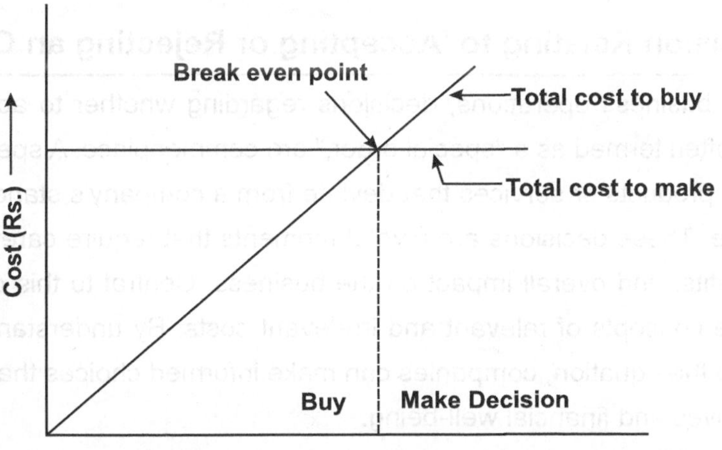

Fig. 1.1 Relationship between Cost to Make and Cost to Buy

E) Illustration :

The total cost of a manufactured component is as under:

Prime cost Rs. 15 Fixed overhead Rs. 4

Variable overhead Rs. 7 Total cost Rs. 26

The same part is available in the market at Rs. 23. Should the firm make it or buy it?

Solution:

If surplus capacity is available and will remain idle if the component is bought, the out of pocket expenses will be Rs. 23 per unit. Re. 1 more than the variable (relevant) cost of making component which is Rs. 22 (Rs. 15 + Rs. 7). Hence, it is economical to make it. However, if the firm is utilizing or can utilize the capacity in making some other part which contributes, says Rs. 4 per unit, the effective cost of buying the component will be Rs. 19 (Rs. 23 less Rs. 4 contribution from other product). In that case, it would be economical to buy the component at Rs. 23 per unit from outside. The relevant computations for taking decision may be as follows:

	Make	**Per unit cost Buy and leave capacity idle**	**Buy and use capacity for other products**
	Rs.	**Rs.**	**Rs.**
Cost of making/buying	(22)	(23)	(23)
Contribution from other product	-	-	4
Net relevant cost	(22)	(23)	(19)

1.4 Decision Relating to 'Accepting or Rejecting an Order' :

In the realm of business operations, decisions regarding whether to accept or reject a specific order, often termed as a "special order," are commonplace. A special order refers to a request for products or services that deviate from a company's standard offerings or pricing structure. These decisions are pivotal moments that require careful evaluation of the costs, benefits, and overall impact on the business. Central to this decision-making process are the concepts of relevant and irrelevant costs. By understanding how these costs factor into the equation, companies can make informed choices that align with their strategic objectives and financial well-being.

1) Importance of Decision-Making in Business :

Decision-making is a fundamental aspect of running any business. From selecting suppliers to determining production levels, every choice made by a company has financial implications. The process of decision-making involves identifying various alternatives, evaluating their pros and cons, and ultimately choosing the option that best aligns with the company's goals. The goal of decision-making is to maximize value while minimizing costs, all while considering both quantitative and qualitative factors.

2) Role of Relevant Costs :

Relevant costs, often referred to as incremental costs, are the key financial elements in the decision-making process. They are expenses that directly influence the outcome of a particular decision. Relevant costs are future-oriented and are crucial for accurately assessing the financial impact of different choices. By focusing on relevant costs, decision-makers can avoid unnecessary complications and ensure that their choices lead to value creation.

In the context of accepting or rejecting an order, relevant costs include those expenses that are directly affected by the decision. These costs can vary depending on whether the order is accepted or rejected. The objective is to consider the additional expenses or savings associated with each alternative and choose the option that maximizes profitability.

C) Examples of Relevant Costs in Order Decisions

1) Direct Materials and Labor :

Consider a manufacturing company that receives a special order for a product. The relevant costs would include the direct materials required for production as well as any additional labor costs.

2) Variable Overhead :

If fulfilling the special order requires using additional resources, the incremental variable overhead costs specific to that order would be relevant.

3) Incremental Shipping Costs :

If the special order involves shipping the product to a different location, any incremental shipping expenses should be included in the calculation.

4) Discounts or Price Reductions :

If the special order is offered at a discounted price compared to the standard offering, the difference in revenue should be considered a relevant cost.

D) Understanding Irrelevant Costs :

Irrelevant costs, on the other hand, are those expenses that do not impact the decision-making process. They are costs that remain constant regardless of the decision taken or costs that are sunk and cannot be recovered. Ignoring irrelevant costs is crucial to ensure that the decision is based on accurate financial considerations and not influenced by factors that do not contribute to the decision's outcome.

E) Examples of Irrelevant Costs in Order Decisions :

1) Sunk Costs :

Sunk costs are expenses that have already been incurred and cannot be recovered. In the context of a special order decision, any costs associated with research and development that were expended before the order was received are irrelevant.

2) Fixed Costs :

Fixed costs, such as rent or salaries, remain constant regardless of the decision. These costs do not change with the acceptance or rejection of a special order and are typically considered irrelevant in this context.

3) Opportunity Costs :

Opportunity costs, while important in other decision scenarios, are generally considered irrelevant in order decisions. This is because they relate to the potential benefits foregone by not choosing a different alternative.

F) The Decision-Making Process for Order Acceptance :

Making a decision regarding whether to accept or reject a special order involves a structured process that considers both relevant and irrelevant costs:

1) Identify the Decision :

Clearly define the decision that needs to be made – whether to accept or reject the special order.

2) Identify Relevant and Irrelevant Costs :

Distinguish between costs that will change based on the decision (relevant costs) and costs that remain constant or have already been incurred (irrelevant costs).

3) Calculate Relevant Costs :

Calculate the relevant costs for each alternative. This entails identifying the incremental expenses or savings associated with each choice.

4) Compare Alternatives :

Compare the relevant costs for accepting the order versus rejecting it. The option with the more favorable financial outcome is the one that should be chosen.

5) Exclude Irrelevant Costs :

Exclude costs that do not impact the decision-making process. Irrelevant costs, such as sunk costs or fixed costs, should not factor into the analysis.

6) Consider Qualitative Factors :

While financial considerations are essential, qualitative factors should also be taken into account. These might include the potential for future business from the client, strategic implications, and reputational effects.

7) Make an Informed Decision :

Based on the analysis of relevant costs, qualitative factors, and the overall strategic direction of the company, make a decision that aligns with the desired outcome.

▶ 1.5 Extra Shift Decision :

In the dynamic landscape of business operations, decisions regarding whether to add an extra shift are significant and multifaceted. An extra shift entails extending the operating hours beyond the standard schedule to meet increased demand, improve efficiency, or respond to changing market conditions. This decision, like many others in business, necessitates a comprehensive analysis that takes into account relevant and irrelevant costs, as well as a broader evaluation of strategic implications. By understanding the intricacies of this decision-making process, companies can optimize their resource utilization, enhance productivity, and maximize profitability.

A) Understanding the Importance of Extra Shift Decisions :

The decision to add an extra shift is a strategic one that can impact various aspects of a business, including production capacity, labor costs, customer satisfaction, and overall financial performance. Companies often face the challenge of managing fluctuating demand, and the decision to extend operating hours can provide a competitive advantage by meeting customer needs more effectively. However, this decision must be balanced with considerations of costs and potential benefits.

B) The Role of Relevant Costs in Extra Shift Decisions :

Relevant costs, also known as incremental costs, play a pivotal role in evaluating the viability of adding an extra shift. These are expenses that change as a direct result of the decision and are therefore vital in determining the financial implications. Relevant costs help decision-makers assess whether the potential benefits outweigh the additional expenses associated with the extra shift. In the context of an extra shift decision, relevant costs encompass various elements:

1) Labor Costs :

If the extra shift requires hiring additional employees or paying overtime to existing staff, the incremental labor costs would be a key relevant cost.

2) Operating Costs :

Expenses related to utilities, equipment usage, and materials required during the extended shift are also relevant costs.

3) Administrative Costs :

If the extra shift leads to increased administrative expenses, such as management and supervisory salaries, these would be included in the analysis.

4) Overhead Costs :

Variable overhead costs that vary with the extended hours of operation are relevant in the decision-making process.

C) Examples of Relevant Costs in Extra Shift Decisions :

1) Overtime Wages :

Consider a manufacturing company contemplating an extra shift. The relevant costs would include the additional wages paid to employees working during the extended hours.

2) Energy Usage :

If running an extra shift requires increased energy consumption, the incremental energy costs would be relevant.

3) Raw Materials :

If the production process during the extra shift consumes more raw materials, the additional materials costs would be a relevant expense.

D) Understanding Irrelevant Costs in Extra Shift Decisions :

Irrelevant costs are those that do not directly impact the decision-making process. These are costs that remain constant regardless of the decision taken or costs that have already been incurred. Irrelevant costs should be excluded from the analysis to ensure that the decision is based on accurate financial considerations.

In the context of an extra shift decision, identifying and excluding irrelevant costs is essential to prevent distorted conclusions.

E) Examples of Irrelevant Costs in Extra Shift Decisions :

1) Sunk Costs :

Any costs that have been incurred in the past and cannot be recovered, such as research and development costs, are irrelevant to the decision of adding an extra shift.

2) Fixed Costs :

Fixed costs that do not change with the addition of an extra shift, such as rent or annual salaries, are typically considered irrelevant in this context.

3) Opportunity Costs :

While important in other scenarios, opportunity costs (the value of the next best alternative) are usually considered irrelevant in the context of adding an extra shift.

F) The Decision-Making Process for Adding an Extra Shift :

The process of deciding whether to add an extra shift involves several systematic steps:

1) Identify the Decision :

Clearly define the decision to add an extra shift and determine the purpose behind the decision (meeting demand, improving efficiency, etc.).

2) Identify Relevant and Irrelevant Costs :

Differentiate between costs that will change based on the decision (relevant costs) and costs that remain constant or have no impact (irrelevant costs).

3) **Calculate Relevant Costs :**
   Calculate the relevant costs associated with the extra shift. This involves identifying the incremental expenses directly tied to the extended hours.

4) **Compare Alternatives :**
   Compare the relevant costs of adding an extra shift with the potential benefits and revenue generation it offers. Assess whether the financial outcome justifies the additional expenses.

5) **Exclude Irrelevant Costs :**
   Exclude costs that do not influence the decision. Focus solely on the costs that change with the extra shift.

6) **Consider Qualitative Factors :**
   While financial considerations are crucial, qualitative factors such as employee morale, customer satisfaction, and the impact on overall business operations should also be evaluated.

7) **Make an Informed Decision :**
   Based on the analysis of relevant costs, qualitative factors, and the strategic alignment of the decision, make a well-informed choice regarding whether to add the extra shift.

1.6 Decision Relating to 'Choosing best budget using only one Limiting Factor' :

In the realm of budgeting and resource allocation, decisions are frequently shaped by various constraints and limitations. When faced with the challenge of choosing the best budget using only one limiting factor, a meticulous analysis is required to ensure optimal resource utilization and alignment with overarching goals. The process involves identifying relevant and irrelevant costs, quantifying potential benefits, and strategically allocating resources to achieve the desired outcomes.

A) The Importance of Budgeting Decisions :

Budgeting decisions are the cornerstone of effective financial management. Organizations and individuals must allocate limited resources – be it time, money, or manpower – to various activities, projects, or departments. These decisions determine the allocation of resources to maximize value creation and achieve long-term objectives. When a single limiting factor comes into play, decision-making becomes particularly nuanced, as it requires balancing priorities and optimizing resource utilization within the confines of the constraint.

B) Understanding the Role of Relevant Costs :

Relevant costs, also known as incremental costs, play a pivotal role in shaping budgeting decisions constrained by a single factor. These costs directly influence the outcome of the decision and are essential for evaluating the financial implications of different choices. By focusing on relevant costs, decision-makers can ensure that their choices are based on accurate and meaningful financial considerations.

In the context of choosing the best budget under a single limiting factor, relevant costs encompass expenses that are directly impacted by the constraint. These costs provide insights into the incremental expenses or savings associated with each budget option.

C) Examples of Relevant Costs in Budgeting Decisions :

1) Labor Costs :

Imagine a manufacturing company with limited production capacity due to a lack of skilled labor. In this scenario, relevant costs would include the wages and benefits of additional skilled workers needed to maximize production within the labor constraint.

2) Material Costs :

If a business faces a constraint in terms of available raw materials, the relevant costs would involve the incremental expenses associated with acquiring additional materials or optimizing material usage.

3) Machine Hours :

Consider a scenario where a company's production is constrained by the availability of specific machinery. Relevant costs here would encompass the expenses associated with operating and maintaining the machinery to maximize output.

D) Understanding Irrelevant Costs :

Irrelevant costs are those expenses that do not directly impact the decision-making process. These costs remain constant or have no influence on the choice made. Excluding irrelevant costs from the analysis is essential to ensure that the decision is based solely on factors that contribute to the desired financial outcomes.

In the context of budgeting decisions constrained by a single factor, the identification and exclusion of irrelevant costs prevent skewed conclusions.

E) Examples of Irrelevant Costs in Budgeting Decisions :

1) Sunk Costs :

Costs that have already been incurred in the past and cannot be recovered are irrelevant to the decision at hand. These costs should not influence the choice of the best budget.

2) Fixed Costs :

Fixed costs that remain consistent regardless of the budget choice are typically considered irrelevant in this context. These costs do not change with the varying levels of resources allocated.

F) The Decision-Making Process for Selecting the Best Budget :

The process of choosing the best budget when constrained by a single limiting factor involves several systematic steps:

1) Identify the Constraint :

Clearly define the single limiting factor that is driving the budget decision. This could be a shortage of labor, raw materials, machine capacity, or any other resource.

2) Identify Relevant and Irrelevant Costs :

Distinguish between costs that will change based on the budget choice (relevant costs) and costs that remain constant or have no impact (irrelevant costs).

3) Calculate Relevant Costs :

Calculate the relevant costs associated with each budget option. This involves identifying the incremental expenses or savings tied to the constraint.

4) Quantify Potential Benefits :

Consider the potential benefits associated with each budget option. These benefits could include increased production, improved efficiency, or enhanced revenue generation.

5) Compare Budget Options :

Compare the relevant costs of each budget option with the corresponding potential benefits. Assess which budget choice offers the best financial outcome given the constraint.

6) Exclude Irrelevant Costs :

Exclude costs that do not influence the decision. Focus exclusively on costs that change with the budget choice and directly impact the constraint.

7) Consider Qualitative Factors :

While financial considerations are crucial, qualitative factors such as customer satisfaction, employee morale, and long-term strategic alignment should also be evaluated.

8) Make an Informed Decision :

Based on the analysis of relevant costs, potential benefits, qualitative factors, and alignment with strategic goals, make an informed choice on the best budget option.

1.7 Decision Relating to 'Adding or Deleting Departments or Products' :

In the dynamic landscape of business operations, decisions regarding whether to add or delete departments or products are pivotal and far-reaching. These choices reflect a company's adaptability, responsiveness to market demands, and strategic vision. Such decisions require a meticulous examination of relevant and irrelevant costs, alongside an understanding of qualitative factors that influence market positioning, customer satisfaction, and long-term sustainability.

A) The Significance of Adding or Deleting Departments or Products :

The decision to add or delete departments or products is a strategic endeavor that shapes a company's trajectory. These decisions can lead to enhanced profitability, streamlined resource allocation, and a sharper market focus. Adding a department or product might diversify a company's offerings, cater to emerging trends, or tap into new customer segments. Conversely, deleting a department or product could result from declining demand, changing consumer preferences, or the need to optimize operational efficiency.

B) The Role of Relevant Costs :

Relevant costs, also known as incremental costs, play a pivotal role in the decision-making process of adding or deleting departments or products. These costs are expenses that directly influence the outcome of a specific decision. By focusing on relevant costs, decision-makers can gauge the financial implications of different choices and align them with their business objectives.

In the context of adding or deleting departments or products, relevant costs encompass expenses that vary based on the decision. These costs provide insights into the incremental expenses or savings associated with each choice. By evaluating relevant costs, businesses can make informed decisions that optimize resource utilization and drive profitability.

C) Examples of Relevant Costs in Department/Product Decision :

1) Adding a Department/Line of Products :

Imagine a retail company considering adding a new line of electronic gadgets. The relevant costs would include expenses such as purchasing inventory, marketing, and additional labor for managing the new line.

2) Deleting a Department/Discontinuing a Product :

Consider a manufacturing company contemplating discontinuing a product due to declining sales. Relevant costs here would involve costs associated with winding down production, disposing of existing inventory, and managing employee transitions.

D) Understanding Irrelevant Costs :

Irrelevant costs are those expenses that do not directly impact the decision-making process. These costs remain constant or have no bearing on the choice made. Excluding irrelevant costs from the analysis is essential to ensure that decisions are based on accurate financial considerations. In the context of department or product decisions, the identification and exclusion of irrelevant costs help decision-makers focus on factors that drive value creation.

E) Examples of Irrelevant Costs in Department/Product Decision :

1) Sunk Costs :

Costs that have already been incurred and cannot be recovered are irrelevant to the decision. Previous expenses on research and development or initial setup that do not impact the current choice should not influence the decision.

2) Fixed Costs :

Fixed costs that remain consistent regardless of the decision are typically considered irrelevant in this context. These costs do not change with the addition or deletion of departments or products.

F) The Decision-Making Process for Adding or Deleting Departments/Products :

The process of deciding whether to add or delete departments or products involves systematic steps:

1) Identify the Decision :

Clearly define the decision to add or delete a department or product. Understand the underlying market trends, customer preferences, and overall business strategy.

2) Identify Relevant and Irrelevant Costs :

Distinguish between costs that will change based on the decision (relevant costs) and costs that remain constant or have no impact (irrelevant costs).

3) Calculate Relevant Costs :

Calculate the relevant costs associated with each option. This entails identifying the incremental expenses or savings tied to the decision.

4) Quantify Potential Benefits :

Consider the potential benefits associated with each option. These benefits could include increased revenue, improved operational efficiency, or enhanced market positioning.

5) Evaluate Market and Customer Trends :

Analyze market trends and customer preferences to understand the potential demand for the new department or product or the reasons for discontinuing an existing one.

6) Compare Options :

Compare the relevant costs of adding or deleting departments or products with the corresponding potential benefits. Assess which choice aligns with business objectives and offers the most favorable financial outcome.

7) Consider Qualitative Factors :

While financial considerations are crucial, qualitative factors such as market positioning, customer satisfaction, and long-term business strategy should also be evaluated.

8) Make an Informed Decision :

Based on the analysis of relevant costs, potential benefits, qualitative factors, and alignment with strategic goals, make an informed choice on whether to add or delete the department or product.

Problems on Decision Making

Problem 1 :

Suresh Ltd. is producing a part at a cost of Rs. 11 per unit. The composition of the cost is as follows:

	(Rs.)
Materials	3.00
Wages 4.00	
Overheads–Variable	2.50
Fixed	1.50
	11.00

Presently, the firm has been incurring a total fixed cost of Rs. 15,000 for manufacturing the current production of 10,000 units. An outsider is offering the same component, in all aspects identical in features, for Rs. 10 per unit. On enquiry, it is found from the firm that the machine that is manufacturing the parts would remain idle as the machinery cannot be utilized elsewhere.

A) Should the offer be accepted?

B) Would your answer would be different, if the outside firm reduces the price to Rs. 9, after negotiation. What is the impact of the fixed costs in the decision-making process?

Solution :

The variable cost of the product is as under:

	(Rs.)
Materials	3.00
Wages	4.00
Overheads–Variable	2.50
Total Variable Cost	**9.50**

A) Here, the additional costs (variable costs) for making are Rs. 9.50. The outside market price is Rs. 10. The outside offer is on a higher side by Rs. 0.50 per unit, so the offer is to be rejected. For every unit bought outside, it results in a loss of Rs. 0.50 per unit.

B) Now, the outside firm is willing to reduce the price to Rs. 9, while the variable cost is Rs. 9.50. The offer is to be accepted.

So far as the fixed costs Rs. 15,000 is concerned, the firm would incur, whether the firm makes the product itself or buys it outside. In other words, the existing fixed costs are not to be considered, while taking a decision.

Problem 2 :

Rani and Co. Manufactures automobile accessories and parts. The following are the total processing costs for each unit.

	(Rs.)
Direct material cost	5,000
Direct labour cost	8,000
Variable factory overhead	6,000
Fixed cost	50,000

The same units are available in the local market. The purchase price of the component is Rs. 22,000 per unit. The fixed overhead would continue to be incurred even when the component is bought from outside, although there would be reduction to the extent of Rs. 2,000 per unit. However, this reduction does not occur, if the machinery is rented out.

Required :

A) Should the part be made or bought, considering that the present capacity when released would remain idle?

B) In case, the released capacity can be rented out to another manufacturer for Rs. 4,500 per unit, what should be the decision?

Solution :

A) The present capacity when released would be remain idle:

Statement showing the cost to make or buy

Buy	**Make**		**Buy**
Direct Material	5,000		
Direct Labour	8,000		
Variable Factory Overhead	6,000	19,000	
Purchase price			22,000
Reduction in fixed cost per unit			-2,000
		19,000	20,000

Since the cost to make is less than the price to buy, it is desirable to manufacture the component as the idle capacity is not, alternatively, used.

B) Statement showing costs of two alternatives, when released capacity is rented out :

Cost Element per Unit	Make	Buy
Relevant Cost to Make	19,000	
Purchase Price		22,000
Related income from alternative use per unit		(4,500)
Total Relevant Cost	19,000	17,500

In the above situation, the decision is in favour of buying from outside.

Problem 3 :

Dimpy Co. A radio manufacturing company finds that the existing cost of a component, Z 200, is Rs. 6.25. The same component is available in the market at Rs. 5.75 each, with an assurance of continued supply.

The breakup of the existing cost of the component is:

		Rs.
Materials		2.75 each
Labour	1.75 each	
Other Variables		0.50 each
Depreciation and other Fixed Cost		1.25 each
		6.25 each

a) Should the company make or buy? Present the case, when the firm cannot utilize the capacity elsewhere, profitably, and when the capacity can be utilized, profitably.

b) What would be your decision, if the supplier has offered the component at Rs. 4.50 each?

Solution :

The decision to make or buy will be influenced by the fact whether the capacity to be released, by not manufacture of the component, can be utilized profitably, elsewhere, or not.

If the capacity would be idle:

Fixed costs are sunk costs. These fixed costs cannot be saved, as the capacity cannot be utilized in an alternative way, profitably. Even if the product is purchased, still the firm has to incur fixed costs.

Variable costs per unit, ignoring fixed costs are:

	Rs.
Materials	2.75
Labour	1.75
Other variables	0.50
Total	**5.00**

By incurring Rs. 5, component, Z 200 can be manufactured by the firm, while it is available in the market at Rs. 5.75 each. So, it is desirable for the firm to make.

If the capacity would not be idle:

Capacity that is released would be utilized elsewhere, profitably. So, the costs that can be avoided by buying are both variable costs as well as fixed costs. So, the total costs assume the character of variable costs. Costs that can be saved are

	Rs.
Materials	2.75 each
Labour 1.75 each	
Other Variables	0.50 each
Depreciation and other Fixed Cost	1.25 each
Total	**6.25**

a) The same product is available at Rs. 5.75. So, by buying, instead of making, there is a saving of Rs.0.50 per unit. So, if the capacity would not be idle, it is better to buy rather than making.

b) The marginal cost of the product (only variable expenses) is Rs. 5. If the price offered is Rs. 4.50 per unit, then the offer can be accepted as there will be saving of 50 paise per unit, even if the capacity released cannot be, profitably, employed. This is so because the price offered is less than the marginal cost of the product.

Problem 4 :

Cost of a component "X" and its market price are as under:

Direct Material Rs.	400
Direct Labour Rs.	200
Prime Costs Rs.	600
Overhead Cost Rs.	200 (Fixed Rs. 150 and Variable Rs. 50)
Total Cost Rs.	800
Market Price Rs.	700

The firm is planning to discontinue the production of component "X" and intends to manufacture component "Y" as current market price of "X" is high. Advise the firm about the production if

i) capacity of the plant would remain idle, if "X" is not manufactured and

ii) capacity of the plant, that would be freed, can be utilized profitably, in making component "Y". Advise for any other considerations.

Solution :

i) **Case when the capacity would remain idle :**

The total cost is Rs. 800, while its market price is Rs. 700. Prima facie, it looks it is cheap to buy rather than making the component. However, analysis shows the correct picture is not so. Fixed costs are sunk costs as they are already incurred and cannot be saved, in the short run. In other words, firm would continue to incur fixed costs, whether the firm makes the component or buys it from the market. Firm cannot utilize the capacity that would be freed, elsewhere, and so remains idle. Hence, fixed costs are permanent costs that cannot be saved, if not utilized, elsewhere. So, a real comparison is between the total costs (Rs. 800) and aggregate of market price (Rs. 700) along with the fixed costs (Rs. 150) that cannot be saved. The aggregate is Rs. 850. It is not wise to buy at Rs. 850, which can be made at Rs. 800. So, it is desirable for the firm to continue to make. There is another way to explain. Compare variable costs (Rs. 650) with market price (Rs. 700). It is, now, Marginal Costing. Even in this type comparison too, it is desirable for the firm to continue to make.

ii) Case when the capacity can be utilized, elsewhere :

Here, the capacity can be utilized, profitably, elsewhere. In other words, the existing fixed costs would be recovered by making component "Y". In other words, these fixed costs component of Rs. 150 also can be saved if component "X" is not manufactured. So, total savings are:

Direct Material	Rs. 400
Direct labour	Rs. 200
Prime cost	Rs. 600
Variable Overhead Cost	Rs. 50
Fixed Cost	Rs. 150
Total Cost	Rs. 800

Total costs that can be saved are Rs. 800. The market price is Rs. 700. So, it is desirable to buy at Rs. 700 instead of incurring Rs. 800.

Other Consideration :

Further, irregularity of supplies from the outside source should also be taken into account, which is an important issue to be considered, before a final decision. In case, the supplies from outside are assured, the firm should go for purchase from outside agency.

When capacity can be alternatively utilized, even the fixed costs become variable costs. Total costs that can be saved are to be compared with the market price for deciding, whether to manufacture or buy the component.

Problem 5 :

An umbrella manufacturer makes an average Profit of Rs. 2.50 per units on a selling price of Rs. 14.30 by producing and selling 60000 units at 60% of potential capacity.

His cost of sales per unit is as follows :

Direct materials	Rs. 3.50
Direct Wages	Rs. 1.25
Factory Overhead	Rs. 6.25 (50% Fixed)
Sales Overhead	Rs. 0.80 (25% Variable)

During the current year, he intends to produce the same number but estimates that his fixed cost would go up by 10% while the rates of direct wages and direct materials will increase by 8% and 6% respectively. However, the selling price cannot be changed. Under this situation, he obtains an offer for a further 20% of his potential capacity. What minimum price would you recommend for acceptance of the offer to ensure the manufacturer and overall profit of Rs. 167300/-?

Solution :

Statement of Marginal Cost and Profit for the current year utilizing 60% of potential capacity.

	Per Unit Rs.	For 60,000
	Units	**Rs.**
A. Sales	14.3	8,58,000
B. Variable Cost :		
Direct materials (Rs. 3.50 + 6%)	3.71	2,22,600
Direct Wages (Rs. 1.25 + 8%)	1.35	81,000
Variable Factory Overheads (50% of Rs. 6.25)	3.125	
		1,87,500
Variable Sales Overheads (25 % of Re. 0.80)	0.2	12,000
	8.385	**5,03,100**
C. Contribution (A-B)	5.915	3,54,900
D. Fixed Cost		2,45,850
Profit (C - D)		**1,09,050**

Now, if the new offer is accepted for a further 20% of the potential capacity, then the additional number of units to be produced = 60,000 x 20% / 60% = 20,000 units.

Statement showing computation of recommended minimum price for the offer to ensure an overall profit of Rs. 1,67,300

	Rs.
Variable Cost to be incurred (20,000 units x Rs. 8.385)	1,67,700
Add : Additional Profit to be earned to ensure an Overall Profit (Rs. 1,67,300 - Rs. 1,09,050)	58,250
Recommended total minimum Selling Price for additional 20,000 units	2,25,950
Recommended minimum Selling Price per unit (Rs. 2,25,950/20,000)	11.2975

Working notes :

Calculation of Total Fixed Cost for the current Year

	Rs.
Fixed Factory Overheads [(50% of Rs. 6.25) x 60,000]	1,87,500
Fixed Sales Overheads [(75% of Re. 0.80) x 60,000]	36,000
	2,23,500
Add : 10% in Current Year (10% of Rs. 2,23,500)	22,350
Total Fixed Cost	**2,45,850**

Problem 6 :

A company manufactures and markets three products A, B and C. All the three products are made from the same set of machines. Production is limited by machine capacity. From the data given below, indicate priorities for products A,B and C with a view to maximising profits :

Particulars	Products		
	A (Rs.)	B (Rs.)	C (Rs.)
Raw Material Cost per unit	11.25	16.25	21.25
Direct labour Cost per unit	2.50	2.50	2.50
Other variable Cost per unit	1.50	2.25	3.55
Selling price per unit	25.00	30.00	35.00
Standard machine time required per minutes	39	20	28

Solution :

STATEMENT INDICATING PRIORITIES OF DIFFERENT PRODUCTS TO MAXIMISE PROFITS

Particulars	A		B		C	
	Rs.	Rs.	Rs.	Rs.	Rs.	Rs.
Selling price per unit		25.00		30.00		35.00
Less : Variable Cost per unit :						
Raw Material Cost per unit	11.25		16.25		21.25	
Direct Labour Cost per unit	2.50		2.50		2.50	
Other Variable Cost per unit	1.50	15.25	2.25	21.00	3.55	27.30
i) Contribution per unit		9.75		9		7.70
ii) Standard machine time required per unit in minutes (i ÷ ii)		39.00		20.00		28.00
iii) Contribution per minute		0.25		0.45		0.275
Priorities for products		III		I		II

Problem 7 :

The following particulars are extracted from the records of a company.

Particulars	Per Unit	
	Product Alpha	Product Beta
Sale Price (Rs.)	100	110
Consumption of Materials (kg.)	5	4
Material cost (Rs)	24	14
Direct wages (Rs.)	2	3
Machine hours used	2	3
Variable overheads	4	6

Comment on the profitability of each product (both use the same material) when :

i) Total sales potential in units is limited.

ii) Total sales potential in value is limited.

iii) Raw Material is in short supply.

iv) Production capacity (in terms of machine hour) is the limiting factor.

Solution :

Particulars	Per Unit	
	Product Alpha	Product Beta
	Rs.	Rs.
Sale Price	100	110
Less : Variable cost	30	23
Contribution	70	87
Contribution per rupee of Sales (P/V Ratio)	70 paise	79 paise
Contribution per kg. of Material	Rs. 14	Rs. 21.75
Contribution per machine hour	Rs.35.	Rs. 29.

i) When total sales potential in units is limited, product B will be better as compared to A as its contribution per unit is more by Rs.17(i.e. Rs. 87 - Rs. 70).

ii) When sales potential in value is limited, product B is better as compared to A as its contribution per rupee of sales is more by 9 paise (i.e. 79 paise - 70 paise).

iii) When raw material is in short supply, product B is better as compared to A as its contribution per kg. of material is more by Rs. 7.75 (i.e. Rs. 21.75 - Rs. 14).

iv) When production capacity (in terms of machine hours) is the limiting factor, product A is better as compared to B as its contribution per machine hour is more by Rs. 6(i.e. Rs. 35 - Rs. 29).

Problem 8 :

A company manufactures and markets three products A, B and C. All the three products are made from the same set of machines. Production is limited by machine capacity. From data given below indicate priorities for products A, B, and C with a view to maximising profits.

Particulars	Product A	Product B	Product C
Raw Material Cost per unit	Rs. 2.25	Rs. 3.25	Rs. 4.25
Direct Labour Cost per unit	Re. 0.50	Re.0.50	Re.0.50
Other Variable Cost per unit	Re.0.30	Re.0.45	Re.0.71
Selling Price per unit	Rs.5.00	Rs.6.00	Rs.7.00
Standard machine time required per unit	39 minutes	20 minutes	28 minutes

In the following year the company faces extreme shortage of raw materials. It is noted that 3kg, 4kg and 5 kg of raw materials are required to produce one unit of A, B and C respectively. How would products priorities change?

Solution :

	Products					
Particulars	A		B		C	
Current year	Rs.	Rs.	Rs.	Rs.	Rs.	Rs.
Selling Price per unit		5.00		6.00		7.00
Less : Marginal cost per unit :						
Raw Materials Cost	2.25		3.25		4.25	
Direct Labour Cost	0.5		0.5		0.5	
Other Variable Cost	0.3		0.45		0.71	
		3.05		4.20		5.46
i) Contribution per unit		1.95		1.80		1.54
ii) Standard machine time required per unit (Minutes)		39		20		28
Contribution per machine minute i ÷ ii		0.05		0.09		0.055
Priorities for products		III		I		II
following year						
Raw materials required to produce in one unit		3 kg.		4kg.		5 kg.
Contribution per kg. of raw material		65		45		30.8
Priorities for products		I		II		III

Exercise

Problem 1 :

In a purely competitive market 10000 units of a product can be manufactured and sold and a certain amount of profit is generated. It is estimated that 2000 units of that product need to be manufactured and sold in a monopoly market to earn the same amount of profit. Profit under both the market conditions is targeted at Rs. 200000. The variable cost per unit is Rs. 100 and the total fixed cost is Rs. 60000. You are required to determine the selling prices under both monopoly and competitive conditions.

Problem 2 :

From the following information you are required to show clearly to management: (i) the marginal cost and the contribution per unit; (II) the total contribution and profits resulting from each of the following sales mixes:

	Product A (Rs.)	Product B (Rs.)
Fixed expenses Rs. 800 p.a.		
Direct Materials per unit	10	9
Direct wages per unit	3	12
Variable overhead (100% of Direct wages)		
Selling price per unit	20	15

Sales mixes:

a) 100 units of product A and 200 units of B

b) 150 units of product A and 150 units of B

c) 200 units of product A and 100 units of B Recommend which of the above sales mixes should be adopted.

Problem 3 :

Spark Ltd. manufactures automobile parts. The following costs are incurred for making 100000 parts by utilizing its in-house production facilities:

	Amount
Direct material cost	7,00,000
Direct labour cost	5,00,000
Direct expenses	3,50,000
Factory overhead (variable portion)	5,50,000
Factory overhead (fixed portion)	7,50,000

The company considers purchasing of automobile parts from outside supplier at a price of 24 per unit. Should the company make or buy the automobile parts?

Problem 4 :

Sturdy Ltd. has been considering installation of a new machine from the available two alternatives. Both the machines can produce more or less the same quality product. The following two alternative methods of production are to be considered for decision making purpose:

Particulars	Machine - X	Machine - Y
Initial cost of machine	30,00,000	20,00,000
Life of machines	10 Years	8 Years
Scrap value	NIL	NIL
Fixed overhead per year (other than Depreciation)	6,00,000	4,00,000
Output per year	25,000 units	20,000 units
Variable cost per unit	40	50
Selling price per unit	90	90

Depreciation is to be charged on Straight line basis. Assume that there is huge demand for the product in the market.

Which machine would you like to select?

Problem 5 :

Management of PQR Ltd. which is now operating at 60°/o of normal capacity expects that the volume of sale will drop below the present level of 6000 units per month. The income statement for monthly sales shows the following position:

	Rs.
Sales (6000 units @ Rs. 4 per unit)	24,000
Variable costs	16,000
Contribution	8,000
Less : Fixed cost	8,000
Profit	NIL

It is proposed that the company should suspend production until market conditions improve. The General Manager estimates that a minimum fixed cost (shut down cost) amounting to Rs. 3200 will be necessary in any event. Advice the management at what level of sales it should think of suspending production,if the selling price comes down to Rs. 3.75 per unit?

Multiple Choice Questions

1) Opportunity cost refers to the value of the next best alternative that is ------------.

a) chosen b) ignored

c) financially rewarding d) unknown

2) Sunk costs are expenditures that have already been made and cannot be ------------.

a) anticipated b) justified c) avoided d) recouped

3) When comparing different options, marginal cost is the additional cost incurred from producing or consuming ------------ unit(s) of a good or service.

a) fewer b) identical c) more d) dissimilar

4) Fixed costs are expenses that remain constant regardless of ------------ produced or sold.

a) profits b) demand c) innovations d) uncertainties

5) Variable costs change in direct proportion to the ------------ of units produced or sold.

a) location b) complexity c) market demand d) quantity

6) Explicit costs are tangible, measurable expenses such as wages and ------------.

a) goodwill b) opportunity costs

c) depreciation d) inspiration

7) Implicit costs are the ------------ costs of using resources that could be employed elsewhere.

a) tangible b) hidden b) external d) specialized

8) Economic costs include both ------------ costs and implicit costs, providing a comprehensive view of expenses.

a) fixed b) variable c) explicit d) external

9) Marginal cost represents the additional cost incurred when producing or consuming ------------ unit(s) of a product or service.

a) fixed b) the first c) previous d) fewer

10) Differential or incremental costs refer to the difference in total costs between two ------------.

a) identical products b) time periods

c) alternatives d) industries

11) Opportunity cost is the value of the next best alternative foregone when a decision involves ------------.

a) low risk
b) personal preferences
c) multiple variables
d) scarce resources

12) Out-of-pocket costs encompass the actual monetary expenses incurred in a decision, including ------------.

a) fixed costs
b) variable costs
c) tangible assets
d) intangible benefits

13) Replacement cost represents the expense of replacing an asset at ------------.

a) historical cost
b) market value
c) original cost
d) nominal value

14) Imputed costs are not actual expenses but are assigned to resources based on their ------------.

a) historical value
b) market demand
c) opportunity cost
d) replacement cost

15) Sunk cost refers to a cost that has already been incurred and ------------.

a) is relevant for future decisions
b) can be recovered
c) should be avoided
d) is independent of decisions

16) Committed cost is a type of cost that results from decisions made in the ------------ and cannot be easily changed.

a) short term
b) past
c) present
d) unpredictable future

17) Relevant costs are those costs that directly impact ----------- decision-making process.

a) historical
b) every
c) the future
d) trivial

18) Irrelevant costs are expenses that do not affect the outcome of a ------------.

a) financial statement
b) strategic decision
c) tax calculation
d) short-term project

19) Types of relevant costs include ------------.

a) fixed costs only
b) historical costs
c) opportunity costs and sunk costs
d) imputed costs

20) Types of irrelevant costs encompass ------------.

a) variable costs only
b) committed costs
c) differential costs
d) sunk costs

21) The key difference between relevant and irrelevant costs lies in their impact on the ------------ of a decision.

a) taxation b) timing c) clarity d) outcome

22) Decisions based on relevant costs focus on evaluating choices that consider ------------.

a) past trends b) all available data

c) only fixed costs d) future revenues and costs

23) Decisions based on irrelevant costs might lead to suboptimal choices due to the neglect of ------------ factors.

a) qualitative and quantitative b) historical

c) imputed d) short-term

24) Relevant costs are crucial in making decisions such as ------------.

a) evaluating long-term investments b) assessing sunk costs

c) analyzing historical trends d) focusing on irrelevant data

25) The make or buy decision involves choosing whether to produce a product or ------------ from an external source.

a) improve quality b) diversify operations

c) outsource d) delay production

26) In the make or buy decision, the relevant costs include ------------.

a) future market trends b) historical data

c) sunk costs d) industry regulations

27) When deciding to accept or reject an order, relevant costs include ------------.

a) variable costs b) historical costs

c) imputed costs d) fixed overhead costs

28) Opportunity costs are important to consider when accepting or rejecting an order because they relate to ------------.

a) financial statements b) future orders

c) regulatory compliance d) employee morale

29) In the extra shift decision, if incremental revenue exceeds ------------ taking the extra shift may be beneficial.

a) imputed costs b) total fixed costs

c) historical data d) variable costs

30) The extra shift decision involves evaluating whether the additional costs of running the shift are justified by the ------------.

a) total fixed costs b) incremental revenue

c) industry norms d) employee preferences

31) When facing multiple budget options with a single limiting factor, the best choice maximizes ------------.

a) sunk costs b) fixed costs

c) contribution margin d) historical data

32) The decision to allocate resources based on a limiting factor focuses on optimizing ------------.

a) irrelevant data b) fixed overhead costs

c) resource utilization d) employee satisfaction

33) When making decisions about adding or deleting departments or products, relevant costs include ------------.

a) imputed costs b) historical data

c) opportunity costs d) fixed costs

34) Deciding to add or delete departments or products involves evaluating the impact on overall ------------.

a) industry trends b) employee morale

c) profitability d) historical costs

Ans : **1)** b, **2)** c, **3)** c, **4)** b, **5)** d, **6)** c, **7)** b, **8)** c, **9)** b, **10)** c, **11)** d, **12)** b, **13)** b, **14)** c, **15)** d, **16)** b, **17)** c, **18)** b, **19)** c, **20)** d, **21)** d, **22)** d, **23)** a, **24)** a, **25)** c, **26)** c, **27)** a, **28)** b, **29)**, b, **30)** b, **31)** c, **32)** c, **33)** c, **34)** c.

Review Questions

Q. 1. Concept of Marginal cost for decision making.

Q. 2. Explain the concept of Differential Cost/Incremental Costs.

Q. 3. Explain Opportunity Cost for Decision Making.

Q. 4. What do you understand about relevant cost and irrelevant costs? Give example.

Q. 5. Explain out of Pocket Costs for Decision Making .

Q. 6. Explain the Replacement Costs and Imputed Costs.

Q. 7. Explain the Types of Relevant Cost and Irrelevant Costs.

Q. 8. Explain Make or Buy Decision in brief.

Q. 9. Explain the Decision Relating to 'Accepting or Rejecting an Order'.

Q. 10. Explain the Extra Shift Decision.

Q. 11. Explain the Decision Relating to 'Choosing best budget using only one Limiting Factor'.

Q. 12. Explain the Decision Relating to 'Adding or Deleting Departments or Products'.

Q. 13. Write a short note on following :

a) Sunk Cost.

b) Committed Cost.

c) Difference between Relevant Cost and Irrelevant Costs.

d) Importance of Budgeting Decisions.

e) Factors Influencing on Make or Buy Decision.

❁❁❁❁❁❁

UNIT 2

Activity Based Costing

Introduction :

Activity based costing system is a powerful tool for measuring performance. It helps to identify, describe and assign costs, besides controlling and computing true cost of a product or service and suggests ways to management for cost control. Under the activity based costing (ABC) system, the focus lies on activities performed to produce the products as the cost is first traced to these activities and then to the products. In this system, first of all cost is assigned to activities, which is a real cause of the overheads and then the cost of those activities is assigned to the products on the basis of cost drivers for calculating the costs accurately.

2.1 Activity Based Costing :

Traditionally, cost accountants had arbitrarily added a broad percentage of expenses into the indirect cost. However as the percentages of indirect or overhead costs had risen, this technique became increasingly inaccurate because the indirect costs were not caused equally by all the products. For example, one product might take more time in one expensive machine than another product, but since the amount of direct labour and materials might be the same, the additional cost for the use of the machine would not be recognised when the same broad 'on-cost' percentage is added to all products. Consequently, when multiple products share common costs, there is a danger of one product subsidising another.

2.1.1 Meaning :

Activity Based Costing (ABC) is that costing in which costs begin with tracing of activities and then to producing the product. In other words, it is the process of costing system which focuses on activities performed to produce products. This system assumes that activities are responsible for the incurrence of costs and products create the demand for activities. Costs are charged to products based on individual product's use of each activity. ABC aims at identifying as many costs as possible to be subsequently accounted as direct cost of production. Any cost that is traced to a particular product via its consumption of activity becomes direct of the product. For instance, in conventional costing system, cost of setup and adjustment time is considered as factory overhead and subsequently assigned to different products on the basis of direct labour hours. But in Activity-Based Costing, setup and adjustment time is determined for each product and its costs are directly charged to each product. Thus, by emphasising activities, ABC tries to ascertain the factors that cause each major activity, cost of such activities and the relationship between activities and products produced.

2.1.2 Definitions :

Definition of Activity Based Costing are as follows :

1) **The terminology of CIMA :**

   "A technique of cost attribution to cost units on the basis of benefits received from indirect activities e.g., ordering, setting up, assuring quality."

2) **Horngreen Dasar :**

   "Activity-based costing (ABC) is a system that focuses on activities as fundamental cost objects and utilises cost of these activities as building blocks or compiling the costs of other objects."

2.1.3 Nature of Activity Based Costing :

Activity-Based Costing recognizes that not all costs can be accurately allocated using a single cost driver, such as direct labor hours or machine hours. Instead, ABC identifies multiple cost drivers that more accurately represent the consumption of resources by different activities involved in the production process. This approach enhances the understanding of cost structures by revealing how various activities contribute to the overall costs.

1) **Resource Consumption Focus:**

a) ABC is centered around understanding how different activities within an organization consume resources.

b) It identifies the relationship between activities and the resources they require to operate effectively.

2) **Multiple Cost Drivers:**

a) Unlike traditional costing methods that often rely on a single cost driver (e.g., direct labor hours), ABC considers multiple cost drivers.

b) Various activities may have distinct drivers that better capture their resource consumption patterns.

3) **Activity Hierarchy:**

a) ABC categorizes activities into different levels: unit-level, batch-level, product-level, and facility-level.

b) This hierarchy helps differentiate between activities that directly impact products and those that support broader operations.

4) **Accurate Cost Allocation:**

a) ABC aims to allocate costs more accurately by attributing overhead expenses to specific activities.

b) This precision leads to a better understanding of the true cost of producing products or services.

5) **Identification of Cost Pools:**

a) ABC groups costs into cost pools based on common activities.

b) These cost pools enable the organization to track expenses associated with various activities.

6) **Cost-Effectiveness Emphasis:**

a) ABC highlights the cost-effectiveness of activities and processes.

b) It prompts organizations to analyze which activities are necessary and which could be streamlined or eliminated.

7) **Focus on Value-Added Activities:**

a) ABC helps identify value-added and non-value-added activities.

b) By distinguishing between these activities, organizations can concentrate resources on tasks that directly contribute to customer value.

8) **Enhanced Decision-Making:**

a) ABC provides more accurate and detailed information for decision-making.

b) Managers can make informed choices about pricing, product mix, resource allocation, and process improvements.

9) **Insight into Customer Profitability:**

a) With ABC, organizations can assess the profitability of individual customers or segments.

b) This information guides strategies for customer relationship management and customization of offerings.

10) Process Improvement Tool:

a) ABC serves as a tool for process improvement by highlighting areas with inefficient resource consumption.

b) Organizations can optimize operations by targeting improvements in resource-intensive activities.

11) Product Cost Transparency:

a) ABC reveals the true cost structure of products and services.

b) It helps in setting accurate prices that account for all relevant costs, ensuring profitability.

12) Strategic Planning Aid:

a) ABC supports strategic planning by offering insights into the organization's cost structure.

b) It assists in aligning resources with strategic goals and adapting to changing market conditions.

13) Challenges in Implementation:

a) ABC implementation requires detailed data collection and analysis.

b) It can be more time-consuming and complex compared to traditional costing methods.

14) Customization Possibilities:

a) Organizations can customize the ABC approach to fit their specific needs and industry requirements.

b) This adaptability makes ABC applicable to various sectors and businesses.

15) Technological Integration:

a) Advances in technology have facilitated the implementation and maintenance of ABC systems.

b) Software tools can assist in data collection, cost calculation, and reporting.

16) Alignment with Lean and Six Sigma:

a) ABC complements Lean and Six Sigma methodologies by providing a detailed understanding of resource consumption.

b) It aids in identifying waste and inefficiencies targeted by these continuous improvement strategies.

In summary, Activity-Based Costing is a sophisticated costing method that recognizes the relationship between activities, resources, and costs. Its nature lies in its ability to accurately allocate costs, enhance decision-making, identify inefficiencies, and provide valuable insights for strategic planning.

2.1.4 Scope of Activity Based Costing :

The scope of Activity-Based Costing (ABC) extends across various industries, sectors, and organizational functions. Its applicability is not limited to a particular type of business;

instead, it offers valuable insights and benefits to organizations of varying sizes and complexities. Below are some of the key areas where ABC finds its scope:

1) **Manufacturing :**

   ABC is widely used in manufacturing industries to better understand the cost structure of different products. It helps manufacturers allocate costs more accurately based on the specific activities that drive those costs. This information aids in making informed decisions about product pricing, process improvements, and resource allocation.

2) **Service Industry :**

   In service-oriented businesses, such as healthcare, consulting, legal services, and financial services, ABC is applied to allocate costs to different services offered. This enables organizations to determine the profitability of each service, optimize resource allocation, and improve service delivery efficiency.

3) **Retail and Distribution :**

   Retailers use ABC to analyze the costs associated with different product lines, brands, or distribution channels. This insight helps in inventory management, assortment planning, and pricing strategies to maximize profitability.

4) **Healthcare :**

   Hospitals and healthcare providers employ ABC to determine the true costs of medical procedures, treatments, and patient services. This information assists in pricing services accurately, optimizing resource utilization, and identifying areas for cost reduction.

5) **Government and Public Services :**

   Government agencies use ABC to assess the cost of providing public services such as education, public safety, and transportation. This allows for better resource allocation, budgeting, and transparency in resource utilization.

6) **Financial Services :**

   Banks, insurance companies, and other financial institutions utilize ABC to allocate costs to different products and services, such as banking services, insurance policies, and investment products. This aids in pricing, profitability analysis, and strategic decision-making.

7) **Utilities :**

   Energy, water, and other utility companies can apply ABC to understand the cost of providing services to different customers, usage patterns, or geographic regions. This information helps in optimizing resource allocation and pricing structures.

8) **Telecommunications :**

   Telecom companies use ABC to allocate costs to different services, such as voice, data, and internet, and determine the profitability of each service. This insight guides pricing strategies and investment decisions.

9) Project-Based Organizations :

Organizations that work on projects, such as construction companies or consulting firms, benefit from ABC by allocating costs to specific projects based on the activities involved. This helps in evaluating project profitability and making resource allocation decisions.

10) Nonprofit Organizations :

Nonprofits can use ABC to understand the cost of various programs and services they offer. This helps in effective resource allocation, fundraising decisions, and accountability to donors and stakeholders.

11) Strategic Decision-Making :

Beyond specific industries, ABC's scope extends to strategic decision-making across various functions, including product development, process improvement, capacity planning, and market expansion. It provides valuable insights into how different activities impact costs and profitability.

2.2 Difference between Traditional Costing and Activity Based Costing :

Difference between Traditional Costing and Activity Based Costing are as follows :

Points	Activity Based Costing	Traditional Costing
1) Cost Pools	ABC systems accumulate costs into activity cost pools. These are designed to correspond to the major activities or business processes. By design, the costs in each cost pool are largely caused by a single factor the cost driver.	Traditional costing systems accumulate costs into facility-wide or departmental cost pools. The costs in each cost pool are heterogeneous they are costs of many major processes and generally are not caused by a single factor.
2) Allocation Bases	ABC systems allocate costs to products, services, and other cost objects from the activity cost pools using allocation bases corresponding to cost drivers of activity costs.	Traditional systems allocate costs to products using volume-based allocation bases: units, direct labor input, machine hours, revenue dollars.

3) **Hierarchy of Costs**	Allows for non-linearity of costs within the organisation by explicitly recognising that some costs are not caused by the number of units produced.	Generally estimates all of the costs of an organisation as being driven by the volume of product or service delivered.
4) **Cost Objects**	Focuses on estimating the costs of many cost objects of interest: units, batches, product lines, business processes, customers, and suppliers.	Focuses on estimating the cost of a single cost object unit of product or service.
5) **Decision Support**	Because of the ability to align allocation bases with cost drivers, provides more accurate information to support managerial decisions.	Because of the inability to align allocation bases with cost drivers, leads to overcosting and undercosting problems.
6) **Cost Control**	By providing summary costs of organisational activities, ABC allows for prioritisation of cost-management efforts.	Cost control is viewed as a departmental exercise rather than a crossfunctional effort.
7) **Cost**	Relatively expensive to implement and maintain.	Inexpensive to implement and maintain.

2.3 Meaning of terms used in Activity Based Costing :

2.3.1 Activity:

In Activity-Based Costing (ABC), an "activity" refers to a distinct task, process, or operation that consumes resources within an organization. ABC is a cost allocation method that aims to allocate overhead costs more accurately by tracing these costs to the specific activities that drive them. This contrasts with traditional cost allocation methods that may allocate overhead costs based solely on a single cost driver like direct labor hours or machine hours, which can lead to inaccuracies when the relationship between resource consumption and the cost driver is not straightforward.

2.3.2 Cost Objects :

In Activity-Based Costing (ABC), a "cost object" refers to any entity or item for which costs are being measured, allocated, or tracked within an organization. Cost objects help identify the specific items, products, services, or projects that are the focus of cost analysis. By assigning costs accurately to these cost objects, ABC provides a more precise understanding of the true costs associated with various aspects of the organization's operations.

2.3.3 Cost Drivers :

In Activity-Based Costing (ABC), a "cost driver" is a factor that directly influences the consumption of resources and the incurrence of costs within an organization. Cost drivers are used to allocate indirect or overhead costs to specific activities, products, services, or other cost objects. By identifying and measuring the relationship between cost drivers and the consumption of resources, ABC provides a more accurate way to allocate costs compared to traditional methods that rely on arbitrary allocation bases like direct labor hours or machine hours. Cost drivers are essentially the underlying reasons for why certain costs are incurred. They can vary widely depending on the nature of the activities and the organization's operations

2.3.4 Cost Pool :

A cost pool is a grouping or collection of costs that are associated with a particular activity. It's a way of aggregating costs that are related to a common activity type. For instance, if you have various overhead costs related to the setup of machines, you would create a "Setup Cost Pool" to accumulate all costs associated with machine setups.

In the ABC methodology, the relationship between activities and cost pools is essential. Activities drive the costs, and costs are accumulated into cost pools based on the nature of the activity. This allows for a more accurate allocation of costs to products or services that use these activities. The cost pools then contribute to the calculation of cost rates, which are used to allocate costs to products based on their consumption of activities.

2.4 Main Activities and its Cost Drivers :

A case study conducted by J. Innes and F. Mitchell in their Activity Based Cost Management.·A Case Study of Development and Implementation' the main activities and cost drivers are identified as shown in Table.

Main Activities	Main Cost Drivers
1) Customer order processing	Order Value
	Order Source (New / old customer)
	Order source (customer location)
2) Material planning / acquisition	Number of material transactions
	Volume of material receipts
	Volume of material orders

3) Inspection	Inspection plans
	Number of problem suppliers
	Gauge usage
	Lack of good quality
4) Production Control	Engineering Changes
	Supplies performance
	Number of parts operational
	Make versus buy policy
	Number of machine changes
	Order board changes
5) Production	Number to be supervised
	Shift patterns
	Industrial relations issues
	Flow of product from assembly
	Volume of service parts / kit packing
6) Maintenance	Number of machine breakdowns
	Maintenance schedule
	Capital expenditure
	Activity levels
7) Systems	Number of accounting transactions
	Number of systems devices
	Adequacy of existing systems
8) Control Quality	Inspection plans
9) Financial accounting	Number of accounting transactions
	Number of times accounts produced
	Volume of activity
	Co-ordinated shipping process
10) Management accounting	Accuracy of feeder systems
	Management requirements
	Co-operate requirements
	Activity levels
11) Personnel	Recruitment activity
	Industrial relations climate
	Training requirements

2.5 Steps/Stages involved in Activity Based Costing :

Steps that are involved in ABC system are explained as below:

1) **Step 1 : Analysis of Existing Costing System :**

   The costing system that is being operated at present has to be studied and analysed. Necessary alterations have to be carried out so as to accommodate the ABC system.

2) **Step 2: Identification of Activities :**

   After reviewing the existing costing system arises the important task of identifying activities. Preferably a committee comprising of managers from design, manufacturing, distribution, administration and accounting is constituted to identify activities. The committee evaluates a number of activities. For this, a Cost-benefit analysis has to be performed. A few activities which are considered essential are selected. These activities form the basis of activity-based costing system. Cost hierarchy level is to be chosen for each activity.

3) **Step 3: Identification of Products :**

   The next step is to identify the products which are chosen cost objects (products).

4) **Step 4: Identification of Direct Costs of the Products :**

   Direct costs such as direct materials cost, direct manufacturing costs and other direct costs may be identified. The immediate past actual cost may be referred and taken as a yardstick.

5) **Step 5: Selection of Cost Allocation Bases :**

   Identifying the cost allocation bases defines a number of activity pools into which costs must be grouped in activity-based costing system. Cost allocation basis is selected to use for allocating indirect costs to the products. Different activities that have been selected in Step 2 would be taken as bases for allocating indirect costs to products.

6) **Step 6: Identification of Indirect Costs Associated with Cost-Allocation Base :**

   Overhead costs are to be assigned to activities based on cause and effect relationship between the cost-allocation base for an activity and the costs of the activity.

7) **Step 7: Computation of Rate Per Unit of each Cost Allocation Base :**

   Activity-cost rates are to be calculated using the cost-allocation basis, and the indirect costs of each activity are to be computed. This is done by dividing total costs by the quantity of allocation base. Care should be taken in the selection of cost allocation base (e.g., square metre, setup hour, machine hour). Cost hierarchy category should be chosen (output unit level, batch-level, product sustaining and facility sustaining) so as to suit the respective activity. This step is explained in Figure.

Activity : (as in Step 2)

⬇

Choice of Cost Hierarchy Category (Step 2)

⬇

Quantity of Cost Allocation Base (Step 5)

⬇

Determination of Total Costs (Step 6)

⬇

Determination of Overhead Allocation Base (Step 6 + Step 5)

8) **Step 8: Computation of Indirect Costs Allocated to the Products :**

   The total quantity of the cost allocation base used for each activity for each type of product is to be multiplied by the cost allocation rate calculated in the previous step. From this, cost per unit may be computed by dividing this total amount by the quantity of each activity.

9) **Step 9: Computation of total costs of products:**

   Add all the direct costs (calculated as in Step 4) and all indirect costs (calculated as in Step 8) to arrive at the total costs of products.

   The essence of installing an ABC system is as follows:

   a) ABC system identifies all costs used by products. It is immaterial whether the costs are variable or fixed in the short run. It identifies all resources used by products.

   b) While allocating costs to products, choice of hierarchy costs is important. Total costs are first determined by using cost hierarchy level. Then the per-unit costs may be determined by dividing total costs by the number of units produced.

2.6 Steps for Calculating Activity Based Costing for a Product :

Steps for calculating activity based costing for a product are as follows :

1) **Step 1:**

   Identify Activities Identify all the activities involved in the production process and other related processes. Activities are tasks or processes that consume resources, such as setting up machines, processing orders, inspecting products, etc.

2) **Step 2:**

   Determine Cost Drivers For each activity, identify the cost drivers – the factors that influence the cost of that activity. Cost drivers can be various factors like the number of setups, machine hours, orders processed, etc.

3) **Step 3:**
   Assign Costs to Activities Allocate or assign the costs associated with each activity. These costs can include direct costs (like wages of workers performing the activity) and indirect costs (like rent and utilities for the activity's workspace).

4) **Step 4:**
   Calculate Cost Rates For each activity, calculate the cost rate. This is done by dividing the total cost of the activity by the total volume of the cost driver. For example, if the total cost of the setup activity is $10,000 and there were 200 setups, the cost rate for setups would be $50 per setup.

5) **Step 5:**
   Determine Activity Consumption Determine how much of each activity is consumed by each product. This involves analyzing how many times each product requires each activity.

6) **Step 6:**
   Calculate Activity Costs Multiply the consumption of each activity by its corresponding cost rate to calculate the cost of each activity for each product.

7) **Step 7:**
   Calculate Product Costs Sum up the costs of all activities associated with each product to calculate the total cost for each product.

8) **Step 8:**
   Calculate Profit Margins Compare the product costs calculated through ABC with the selling price to calculate the profit margin for each product. This step helps in understanding which products are more profitable based on accurate cost allocation.

9) **Step 9:**
   Evaluate Results Analyze the results of the ABC calculations and compare them with the results obtained through traditional costing. Identify products that were undercosted or overcosted using the traditional method.

10) **Step 10:**
    Implement and Monitor Implement the insights gained from the ABC analysis. This may involve making pricing adjustments, cost-cutting measures, or process improvements based on the more accurate cost information. Continuously monitor and update the ABC system as the business environment changes.

11) **Step 11:**
    Communication and Training Communicate the new cost allocation methodology to relevant stakeholders and provide training to employees who will work with ABC data. This ensures that everyone understands the changes and can use the information effectively.

12) **Step 12:**

Continuous Improvement ABC is not a one-time process. Continuously review and refine the cost drivers, activity definitions, and cost rates as the business evolves and gains a better understanding of its cost structure.

13) **Step 13:**

Software Integration Consider using specialized software to streamline the ABC calculations, especially if your organization has a large number of products and activities. Many software solutions are available that can automate the process and provide detailed reports.

In essence, Activity-Based Costing involves identifying activities, determining their cost drivers, calculating activity costs, and then allocating those costs to products more accurately based on the activities each product consumes. It's a more detailed and sophisticated approach compared to traditional costing, providing better insights into cost structures and aiding in informed decision-making.

2.7 Advantages of Activity Based Costing :

Activity-Based Costing (ABC) is a sophisticated costing methodology that offers numerous advantages for organizations seeking more accurate cost allocation, better decision-making, and improved resource management.

1) **Accurate Cost Allocation:**

ABC provides a more precise method of allocating costs to products, services, or activities. Traditional methods like direct labor or machine hours might inaccurately distribute overhead costs, but ABC uses activity drivers that closely reflect the resource consumption patterns.

2) **Enhanced Cost Visibility:**

ABC uncovers the true costs associated with various activities, allowing organizations to identify cost drivers and understand the relationship between costs and their underlying causes. This transparency helps in making informed decisions.

3) **Improved Decision-Making:**

With accurate cost information, management can make better decisions regarding product pricing, resource allocation, outsourcing, and discontinuing unprofitable products or services.

4) **Optimized Resource Allocation:**

ABC highlights resource-intensive activities, allowing organizations to allocate resources more efficiently. Resources can be focused on activities that provide the most value and eliminate unnecessary tasks.

5) **Better Product Mix Analysis:**
Organizations can analyze the profitability of different product lines or services based on their true costs, assisting in strategic decisions to prioritize or modify offerings.

6) **Customer Profitability Analysis:**
ABC enables the assessment of customer profitability by attributing costs to individual customers or segments. This helps in identifying high-value customers and tailoring strategies accordingly.

7) **Process Improvement Insights:**
By identifying resource-intensive activities and bottlenecks, ABC guides process improvement efforts, leading to streamlined operations, reduced waste, and increased efficiency.

8) **Accurate Budgeting and Planning:**
ABC provides more accurate cost estimates for future activities and projects, leading to improved budgeting and strategic planning.

9) **Fairer Overhead Allocation:**
Traditional costing methods might unfairly allocate overhead costs to certain products or services. ABC allocates costs based on the actual activities driving those costs, resulting in a more equitable distribution.

10) **Enhanced Cost Control:**
The granular view of costs provided by ABC helps organizations monitor and control costs effectively, as it pinpoints areas of excessive spending and guides cost reduction initiatives.

11) **Supports Activity Management:**
Organizations can manage activities more effectively by understanding their cost implications. ABC encourages the assessment of non-value-added activities, which can lead to process simplification and waste reduction.

12) **Catalyst for Continuous Improvement:**
ABC fosters a culture of continuous improvement by encouraging organizations to constantly assess and optimize their processes, leading to ongoing cost savings and operational efficiency gains.

In conclusion, Activity-Based Costing offers a multitude of benefits that range from accurate cost allocation to enhanced decision-making and resource optimization. By providing a more realistic view of the cost structure, ABC empowers organizations to strategically manage their operations and achieve long-term success.

Problems on Activity based Costing

Problem 1 :

The Gadget Co produces three products, A, B and C, all made from the same material. Unit now, it has used traditional absorption costing to allocate overheads to its products. The company is now considering an activity based costing system in the hope that it will improve profitability. Information for the three products for the last year is as follows :

	A	B	C
Production and sales volumes (units)	15,000	12.000	18,000
Selling price per unit	Rs7.50	Rs12	Rs13
Raw material usage(kg) per unit	2	3	4
Direct labour hours per unit	0.1	0.15	0.2
Machine hours per unite	0.5	0.7	0.9
Number of production runs per annum of purchase orders per annum	16	12	8
Number of	24	28	42
Number of deliveries to retailers per annum	48	30	62

The price for raw materials remained constant throughout the year at Rs1.20 per kg. Similarly, the direct labour cost For the whole workforce was Rs14.80 per hour.The annual overhead costs were as follows :

	Rs
Machine set up costs	26,550
Machine running costs	66,400
Procurement costs	48,000
Delivery costs	54,320

Required:

a) Calculate the full cost per unit for products A, B and C under traditional absorption costing, using direct labour hours as the basis for apportionment

b) Calculate the full cost per unit of each product using activity based costing.

c) Using your calculation from (a) and (b) above, explain how activity based costing may help The Gadget Co improve the profitability of each product.

Solution :

a) Cost per unit under full absorption costing

Total annual overhead costs:	**RS**
Machine set up costs	26,550
Machine running costs	66,400
Procurement costs	48,000
Delivery costs	54,320
	195,270

Overhead absorption rate:

	A	B	C	Total
Production volumes	15,000	12,000	18,000	
Labour hours per unit	0.1	0.15	0.2	
Total labour hours	1,500	1,800	3,600	6.900
Therefore, overhead absorption rate-RS195,270/6,900=Rs28.30per hour				

Cost Per Unit :

	A	B	C
	Rs	Rs	Rs
Raw materials (Rs 1.20 x 2/3/4kg)	2.4	3.6	4.8
Direct labour (Rs 14.80x0.1/0.15/0.2hrs)	1.48	2.22	2.96
Overhead (Rs 28.30 x 0.1/0.15/0.2hrs)	2.83	4.25	5.66
Full cost per unit	6.71	10.07	13.42

b) **Cost per Unit using ABC costing :**

Cost drivers:		
Cost pools	**Rs**	**Cost driver**
Machine set up costs	26,550	36 production runs (16+12+8)
Machine running costs	66,400	32,100 machine hours (7,500+8,400+16,200)
Procurement costs	48,000	94 purchase orders (24+28+24)
Delivery costs	54,320	140 deliveries (48+30+62)
	195,270	
Cost per machine set up	Rs. 26,550/36 = Rs. 737.50	
Cost per Machine hour	Rs. 66,400/32,100 = Rs. 2.0685	
Cost per order	Rs. 48,000/94 = Rs. 510.6383	
Cost per delivery	Rs. 54,320/14 = Rs. 388	

Allocation of Overheads to each product :

	A	B	C	Total
	Rs	Rs	Rs	Rs
Machine set up costs	11,800	8,850	5,900	26,550
Machine running cost	15,514	17,375	33,510	66,400
Procurement costs	12,255	14,298	21,447	48,000
Delivery costs	18,624	11,640	24,056	54,320
	58,193	52,163	84,913	1,95,270
Number of units produces	15,000	12,000	18,000	
	Rs	Rs	Rs.	
Overhead cost per unit	3.88	4.35	4.72	
Total cost per unit	A	B	C	
	Rs	Rs	Rs.	
Materials	2.4	3.6	4.8	
Labour	1.48	2.22	2.96	
Overheads	3.88	4.35	4.72	
	7.76	10.17	12.48	

c) **Using activity-based costing :**

When comparing the full unit costs for each of the products under absorption costing as compared to ABC, the following observations can be made :

Product A

The unit cost for product A is 16% higher under ABC asopposed to traditional absorption costing. Under ABC, it is Rs.7·76 per unit compared to Rs.6·71 under traditional costing. This is particularly significant given that the selling price for product A is Rs.7·50 per unit.This means that when the activities that give rise to the overhead costs for product A are taken into account, product A is actually making a loss. If the company wants to improve profit ability it should look to either increase the selling price of product A or some how reduce the costs. Delivery costs are also high, with 48 deliveries a year being made for product A. May be the company could seek further efficiencies here. Also,machine setup costs are higher for product A than for any of the other products, due to the larger number of production runs. The reason for this needs to be identified and, if possible,the number of production runs needs to be reduced.

Product B

The difference between the activity based cost for B as opposed to the traditional cost is quite small, being only Rs.0·10. Since

The selling price for B is Rs.12, product B is clearly profitable which ever method of overhead allocation is used. ABC does not really identify any are as for concern here.

Product C

The unit cost for C is 7% lower under ABC when compared to traditional costing. More importantly, while C looks like it is making a loss under traditional costing, ABS tells a different story. The selling price for C is Rs.13 per unit and, under ABC, it costs Rs.12·48 per unit. Under traditional absorption costing, C is making a loss of Rs.0·42 per unit. Identifying there a son for the differences in C, it is apparent that the number of production runs required to produce C is relatively low compared to the volumes produced. This leads to a lower apportionment of the machine setup costs to C than would be given under traditional absorption costing. Similarly, the number of product tests carried out on C is low relative to its volumes.

ABC is therefore very useful in identifying that C is actually more profitable than A, because of the reasons identified above. The company needs to look at the efficiency that seems to be achieved with C (low number of production runs less testing) and see whether any changes can be made to A, to bring it more in line with C. Of course, this may not be possible, in which case the company may consider whether it wishes to continue to produce A and whether it could sell higher volumes of C.

Problem 2 :

Brick by Brick (BBB) is a building business that provides a range of building services to the public. Recently they have been asked to quote for garage conversions (GC) and extensions to properties (EX) and have found that they are winning fewer GC contracts than expected. BBB has a policy to price all jobs at budgeted total cost plus 50%. Overheads are currently absorbed on a labour hour basis. BBB thinks that a switch to activity based costing (ABC) to absorb overheads would reduce the cost associated to GC and hence make them more competitive.

You are provided with the following data :

Overhead Category	Annual Overheads Rs.	Activity Driver	Total Number of Activities per year
Supervisors	90,000	Site visit	500
Planners	70,000	Planning documents	250
Property related	2,40,000	Labour hours	40,000
Total	**4,00,000**		

A typical GC costs Rs.3,500 in materials and takes 300 labour hours to complete. AGC Requires only one site visit by a supervisor and needs only one planning document to be raised. The typical EX costs Rs.8,000 in materials and takes 500 hours to complete. An EX requires six site visits and five planning documents. In all cases labour is paid Rs. 5 per hour. Rs. Rs.

Required :

a) Calculate the cost and quoted price of a GC and of an EX using labour hours to absorb the overheads.

b) Calculate the cost and the quoted price of a GC and of an EX using ABC to absorb the overheads.

c) Assuming that the cost of a GC falls by nearly 7% and the price of an EX rises by about 2% as a result of the change to ABC, suggest possible pricing strategies for the two products that BBB sells and suggest two reasons other than high prices for the current poor sales of the GC.

d) One BBB manager has suggested that only marginal cost should be included in budget cost calculations as this would avoid the need for arbitrary overhead allocations to products. Briefly discuss this point of view and comment on the implication for the amount of mark-up that would be applied to budget costs when producing quotes for jobs.

Solution :

a) Costs and quoted prices for the GC and the EX using labour hours to absorb overheads :

Materials			**GC Rs**	**EX Rs**
Labour	3000 hrs x Rs 15/hr		3,500	8,000
		5000 hrs x Rs 15/hr	4,500	
Overheads	3000 hrs x Rs 10/hr (W1)			7,500
			3,000	
		5000 hrs x Rs 10/hr		5,000
Total cost			11,000	20,500
Quoted price			16,500	30,750

(W1).Overhead abosorption rate is calculated as Rs4000.000/40,000hrs=Rs10/hr

b) Costs and quoted prices for the GC and the EX using ABC to absorb overheads:

Materials			**GC Rs**	**EX Rs**
Labour	300 hrs x Rs. 15/hr		3,500	8,000
	3000 hrs x Rs. 10/hr (W1)		4,500	
Overheads		5000 hrs x Rs. 15/hr		7,500
-Supervisor	(W2)/(W3)			
-Planners	(W2)/(W3)		180	1,080
-property	(W2)/(W3)		280	1,400
-Supervisor	(W2)/(W3)		1,800	3,000
Total cost			10,260	20,980
Quoted price			15,390	31,470

(W2)

	Costs	Number of drivers	Cost per driver
Supervisor	90,000	500	180
Planners	70,000	250	280
Property	240,000	40,000	6

(W3)

	Supervisor	Planner	Property
Cost per driver (W2)	Rs. 180	Rs. 280	Rs. 6
GC	180 x 1 = 180	280 x 1 = 280	6 x 300 = 1,800
EX	180 x 6 = 1,080	280 x 5 = 1,400	6 x 500 = 3,000

c) The pricing policy is a matter for BBB to decide. They could elect to maintain the current 50% mark-upon cost and if they did the price of the GC would fall by around7% in line with the costs. This should make them more competitive in the market.

They could also reduce the prices by a little less than 7% (say 5%) in order to increase internal margins a little.

It is possible that the issue lies elsewhere. If the quality of the work or the reputation and reliability of the builder is questionable then reducing prices is unlikely to improve sales. It is conceivable that BBB has a good reputation for EX but not for GC, but more likely that a poor reputation would affect all products. Equally poor service levels or lack of flexibility in meeting customer needs may be causing the poor sales performance. These too will not be 'corrected' by merely reducing prices.

It is also possible that the way salesmen discuss or sell their products for the GC is not adequate so that in some way customers are being put off placing the work with BBB.

BBB is in competition and it perhaps needs to reflect this in its pricing more (by 'going rate pricing') and not seek to merely add a mark-up to its costs.

BBB could try to penetrate the market by pricing some jobs cheaply to gain a foothold. Once this has been done the completed EX or GC could be used to market the business to new customers.

The price of the EX would also need consideration. There is no indication of problems in the selling of the EX and so BBB could consider pushing up their prices by around 2% in line with the cost increase. On the figures in my answer the price goes up for a typical extension to Rs.31,470 from Rs. 30,750 arise of Rs.720. This does not seem that significant and so might not lose a significant number of sales.

The reliability and reputation of a builder is probably more important than the price that they charge for a job and so it is possible that the success rate on job quotes may not be that price sensitive.

d) Marginal costs are those costs that are incurred as a consequence of the job being undertaken. In this case they would include only the materials and the labour. If overheads are included then this is known as total absorption costing.

Overheads are for many businesses fixed by nature and hence do not vary as the number of jobs changes. In a traditional sense any attempt to allocate costs to products (by way of labour hours for example) would be arbitrary with little true meaning being added to the end result. The overhead absorption rate (OAR) is merely an average of these costs (over labour hours) and is essentially meaningless. This switch (to marginal costing) would also avoid the problem of the uncertainty of budget volume. Budget volume is needed in order to calculate the fixed cost absorption rate.

The marginal cost (MC) is more understand able by managers and indeed customers and a switch away from total absorption cost (TAC) could have benefits in this way. Clearly if overheads are going to be excluded for the cost allocations then they would still have to be covered by way of a bigger margin added to the costs. In the end all costs have to be paid for and covered by the sales in order to show a profit.

A more modern view point is that activity causes costs to exist. For example, it is the existence of the need for site visits that gives rise to the need for a supervisor and therefore, for his costs. If the activities that drive costs are identified, more costs can then be directly traced to products, hence eradicating the need for arbitrary apportionment of many overhead costs. This has the benefit of all costs being covered, rather than the potential short fall that can a rise if marginal cost plus pricing is used. In the long run businesses have to cover all costs including fixed overheads in order to make a profit, whichever pricing strategy is adopted.

Problem 3 :

Jola Publishing Co publishes two forms of book. The company publishes a children's book (CB), which is sold in large quantities to government controlled schools. The book is produced in only four large production runs but goes through frequent government inspections and quality assurance checks. The paper used is strong, designed to resist the damage that can because by the young children it is produced for. The book has only a few words and relies on pictures to convey meaning.

The second book is a comprehensive technical journal (TJ). It is produced in monthly production runs, 12 times a year. The paper used is of relatively poor quality and is not subject to any governmental controls and consequently only a small number of inspections are carried out. The TJ uses far more machine hours than the CB in its production.

The directors are concerned about the performance of the two books and are wondering what the impact would be of a switch to an activity based costing (ABC) approach to accounting for overheads. They currently use absorption costing, based on machine hours for all overhead calculations. They have accurately produced analysis for the accounting year just completed as follows:

Required:

a) Explain why the overhead allocations have changed in the way indicated above.

b) Briefly explain the implementation problems often experienced when ABC is first introduced.

The directors are keen to introduce ABC for the coming year and have provided the following cost and selling price data:

1. The paper used costs Rs.2 per kg for a CB but the TJ paper costs only Rs.1 per kg. The CB uses 400g of paper for each book, four times as much as the TJ uses.
2. Printing ink costs Rs.30 per litre. The CB uses one third of the printing ink of the larger TJ. The TJ uses 150ml of printing ink per book.
3. The CB needs six minutes of machine time to produce each book, where as the TJ needs 10 minutes per book. The machines cost Rs.12 per hour to run.
4. The sales prices are to be Rs.9·30 for the CB and Rs.14·00 for the TJ

As mentioned above there are three main overheads, the data for these are:

Overhead	Annual cost for the coming year Rs
Property costs	21,60,000
Quality control	6,68,000
Production set up costs	52,000
Total	**28,80,000**

The CB will be inspected on 180 occasions next year, whereas the TJ will be inspected just 20 times. Jola publishing will produce its annual output of 10,00,000 CBs in four production rune and approximately 10,000 TJs per month in each of 12 production runs.

Required:

c) Calculate the cost per unit and the margin for the CB and the TJ using machine hours to absorb the overheads.

d) Calculate the cost per unit and the margin for the CB and the TJ using activity based costing principles to absorb the overheads.

Solution :

a) The first thing to point out is that the overhead allocations to the two products have not changed by that much. For example the CB has absorbed only Rs. 0·05 more overhead. The reason for such a small change is that the overheads are dominated by property costs (75% of total overhead) and the 'driver' for these remains machine hours once the switch to ABC is made. Thus no difference will result from the switch to ABC in this regard.

The major effect on the cost will be for quality control. It is a major overhead (23% of total) and there is a big difference between the relative number of machine hours for each product and the number of inspections made (the ABC driver). The CB takes less time to produce than the TJ, due to the shortness of the book. It will therefore carry a smaller amount of overhead in this regard. However, given the high degree of government regulation, the CB is subject to 'frequent' inspections whereas the TJ is inspected only rarely. This will mean that under ABC the CB will carry a high proportion of the quality control cost and hence change the relative cost allocations.

The production set up costs are only a small proportion of total cost and would be, therefore, unlikely to cause much of a difference in the cost allocations between the two products. However this hides the very big difference in treatment. The CB is produced in four long production runs, whereas the TJ is produced monthly in 12 production runs. The relative proportions of overhead allocated under the two overhead treatments will be very different. In this case the TJ would carry much more overhead under ABC than under a machine hour's basis of overhead absorption.

b) There are many problems with ABC, which, despite its academic superiority, cause issues on its introduction.

- Lack of understanding ABC is not fully understood by many managers and therefore is not fully accepted as a means of cost control.
- Difficulty in identifying cost drivers. In a practical context, there are frequently difficulties in identifying the appropriate drivers. For example, property costs are often significant and yet a single driver is difficult to find.

– Lack of appropriate accounting records. ABC needs a new set of accounting records, this is often not immediately available and therefore resistance to change is common. The setting up of new cost pools is needed which is time consuming.

C) Cost per unit calculation using machine hours for overhead absorption

	Rs CB		Rs TJ
Paper (400 g at Rs 2/ksg)	0.80	(100g at Rs1/kg)	0.10
Printing (50 ml at Rs 30/ltr)	0.15	(150 ml at Rs 30/ltr)	4.50
Machine cost (6 mins at Rs12/hr)	1.20	(10 mins at Rs 12/hr)	2.00
Overheads (6 mins at Rs 24/hr) (W1)	2.40	(10 mins at Rs 24/hr)	4.00
Total cost	5.90		10.60
Sales price	9.30		14.00
Margin	3.40		3.40

(W1) Working for Overheads :

Total Overheads	2,880,000 Rs.
Total machine hours(1,000,000 x 6 mins) + (120,000 x 10 mins) =	7,200,000 mins
Which is cost per hour = $\frac{\text{Rs. 2,880,000}}{\text{1,20,000}}$ = Rs. 24/hr	120,000 hours

Cost per unit calculations under ABC

	CB		TJ
	Rs		Rs
Paper (400 g at Rs. 2/kg)	0.80	(100g at Rs1/kg)	0.10
Printing (50 ml at Rs. 30/ltr)	1.50	(150ml at Rs. 30/ltr)	4.50
Machine cost (6 mins at Rs. 12/hr)	1.20	(10 mins at Rs. 12/hr)	2.00
Overheads (6 mins at Rs. 24/hr) (W1)	2.41	(W2)	.88
Total cost	5.91		10.48
Sales price	9.30		14.00
Margin	3.39		3.52

(W2) Working for ABC overheads

	Total	CB	TJ	No of drivers	Cost/ drivers	CB	TJ
	Rs	Rs	Rs	120,000	18/hr	1.80	3.00
Property cost	21,60,000	18,00,000	360,000	200	3340	0.6012	0.56
Quality control	6,68,000	6,01,200	66,800	16	3250	0.013	0.325
Production set up	52,000	13,000	39,000	Cost per unit		2.41	3.88
Total	28,80,000	24,14,200	4,65,800				
Production level		10,00,000	1,20,000				
Cost per unit		2.41	3.88				

The above Overheads have been split on the basis of the following activity levels

	Driver	CB	TJ
Property costs	Machine hours	1,00,000	20,000
Quality control	Inspections	180	20
Production set up	Set ups	4	12

A Cost per driver approach is also acceptable.

Problem 4 :

Triple Limited makes three types of gold watch–the Diva (D), the Classic (C) and the Poser(P). A traditional product costing system is used at present; although an activity based costing (ABC) system is being considered. Details of the three products for a typical period are:

	Hours per unit		Materials	Production
	Labour hours	**Machine hours**	**Cost per unit (Rs)**	**Units**
Product D	1/2	1 1/2	20	750
Product C	1 1/2	1	15	1,250
Product P	1	3	25	7,000

Total production overheads are Rs 654,500 and further analysis shows that the total production overheads can be divided as follows:

	%
Cost relating to set-ups	35
Cost relating to machinery	20
Cost relating to materials handling	15
Cost relating to inspection	30
Total production overhead	100

The following total activity volumes are associated with each product line for the period as a whole:

	Number of set ups	Number of movements of materials	Number of inspections
	75	12	150
Product D	115	21	180
Product C	480	87	670
Product P	670	120	1,000

Direct labour costs Rs.6 per hour and production overheads are absorbed on a machine hour basis. The overhead absorption rate for the period is Rs.28 per machine hour.

Required:

a) Calculate the cost per unit for each product using traditional methods, absorbing overheads on the basis of machine hours.

b) Calculate the cost per unit for each product using ABC principles (work to two decimal places).

c) Explain why costs per unit calculated under ABC are often very different to costs per unit calculated under more traditional methods. Use the information from Triple Limited to illustrate.

d) Discuss the implications of as witch to ABC on pricing and profitability.

Solution :

1 TRIPLE Limited

a) Traditional cost per unit

	D	C	P
	Rs	Rs	Rs
Material	20	12	25
Labour (Rs6/hour)	3	9	6
Direct costs	23	21	31
Production overhead (Rs. 28/ machine hour)	42	28	84
Total production cost/unit	**65**	**49**	**115**

b) ABC cost per unit

i) Total overheads

These were given at Rs. 654.500

ii) Total machine hours (needed as the driver for machining overhead)

Product	Hours/unit	Production units	Total hours
D	1 1/2	750	1.125
C	1	1,250	1.250
P	3	7,000	21,000
Total machine hours			23,375

iii) Analysis of total overheads and cost per unit of activity

Type of overheads	Driver	%	Total overheads Rs	Level of Driver activity	Cost/ driver
Set-ups	Number of set ups	35	229.075	670	341.90
Machining	Machine hours	20	130.900	23,375	5.60
Materials handling	Material movements	15	98.175	120	818.13
Inspection	Number of Inspections	30	196.350	1,000	196.35
		100	**654,500**		

iv) Total overheads by product and per unit

	Product D		Product C		Product P		Total	
Overhead	Activity	Rs Cost	Activity	Rs Cost	Activity	Rs Cost	Activity	Rs Cost
Set-up	75	25,643	115	39,319	480	164,113	670	2,29,075
Machining	1,125	6,300	1,250	7,000	21,000	117,600	23,375	1,30,900
Material handling	12	9,817	21	17,181	87	71,177	120	98,175
Inspection	150	29,453	180	35,343	670	1,31,554	1,000	1,96,350
Total overhead cost		77,213		98,843		4,84,444		6,54,500
Unite produced		750		1,250		7,000		
Cost per unit		Rs. 94.95		Rs. 79.07		Rs. 69.21		

v) Cost per unit

	D	C	P
	Rs	**Rs**	**Rs**
Direct costs (from (a))	23.00	21.00	31.00
Overhead (from (iv))	94.95	79.07	69.21
	117.95	100.07	100.21

Comment

The Overhead costs per unit are summarised together with volume of production.

Product	D	C	P
Volume	750	1,250	7,000
Conventional Overheads	Rs. 42	Rs. 28	Rs. 84
ABC Overheads	Rs. 95	Rs. 79	Rs. 69

The result of the change to activity based costing is clear, the Overhead cost of D and C have risen whilst that of P has failen.

This is in line with the comments of many who feel that ABC provides a fairer unit cost better reflecting the effort required to

Make different products. This is illustrated here with product P which may take longer to make that D or C, but once production

Has started the process is simple to administer. This may be due to having much longer production line. Products D and C are relatively minor volume products but still require a fair amount of administrative time by the production

Department; ie they involve a fair amount of 'hassle'. This is explained by the following table of 'activities per 1,000 units produced'.

	Set-ups	Materials movements	Inspections
D	100	16	200
C	92	17	144
P	69	12	96

This table highlights the problem:

- Product P has fewer set-ups, material movements and inspections per 1,000 units than or C
- As a consequence product P's overhead cost unit for these three elements has fallen
- The machining overhead cost per unit for P is still two or three time greater than for products D or C, but because this overhead only accounts for 20% of the total overhead this has a small effect on total cost.
- The Overall result is P's fall in production overhead cost per unit and the rise in those figures for D and C

d) Pricing and Profitability

Switching to ABC can, as in this case, substantially change the costs per unit calculations. Consequently if an organisation's selling prices are determined by a version of cost-plus pricing then the selling prices would alter.

In this case the selling price of D and C would rise significantly, and the selling price of P would fall. This, at first glance may be appealing however:

– Will the markets for D and C tolerate a price rise? There could be competition to consider. Will customers be willing to pay more for a product simply because Triple Ltd has changed its cost allocation methods?

– Product P is a high volume product. Reducing its selling price will have a dramatic effect on revenue and contribution. One would have to question whether such a reduction would be compensated for by increased volumes.

Alternatively, one could take the view that prices are determined by the market and there fore if Triple Ltd switches to ABC, it is not the price that would change but the profit or margin per unit that would change. This can change attitudes with in the business. Previously high margin products (under a traditional overhead absorption system) would be shown as less profitable.

Salesmen (possibly profit motivated) can begin to push the sales of different products seeking higher personal rewards. (Assuming commission based on profits per units old)

It must always be remembered that if overheads are essentially fixed then they should be ignored in business decision making. Switching to ABC can change reported profits per unit but it is contribution per unit that is perhaps more important.

Problem 5 :

Duff Co manufactures three products , X , Y and Z . Demand for products X and Y is relatively elastic whilst demand for product Z is relatively inelastic. Each product uses the same materials and the same type of direct labour but in different quantities. For many years, the company has been using full absorption costing and absorbing overheads on the basis of direct labour hours. Selling prices are then determined using cost plus pricing. This is common with in this industry, with most competitors applying a standard mark-up.

Budgeted production and sales volumes for X, Y and Z for the next year are 20,000 units,16,000 units and 22,000 units respectively.

The budgeted direct costs of the three products are shown below:

Product	X	Y	X
	Rs. Per Unit	Rs. Per Unit	Rs. Per Unit
Direct Materials	25	28	22
Direct labour (Rs. 12 per hour)	30	36	24

In the next year, Duff Co also expects to incur indirect production costs of Rs.1,377,400, which are analyzed as follows:

Cost pools	Rs.	.Cost drivers
Machine setup costs	2,80,000	Number of batches
Material ordering costs	3,16,000	Number of purchase orders
Machine running costs	4,20,000	Number of machine hours
General facility costs	3,61,000	Number of machines hours
Total	**1,377,400**	

The following additional data relate to each product:

Product	X	Y	X
Batchsize (units)	500	800	400
	4	5	4
Machine hours per unit	1.5	1.25	1.4

Duff Co wants to boost sales revenue in order to increase profits but its capacity to do this is limited because of its use of cost plus pricing and the application of the standard mark-up. The finance direct or has suggested using activity based costing (ABC) instead of full absorption costing, since this will alter the cost of the products and may therefore enable a different price to be charged.

Required:

a) Calculate the budgeted full production cost per unit of each product using Duff Co's current method of absorption costing. All workings Should be to two decimal places.

b) Calculate the budgeted full production cost per unit of each product using activity based costing .All workings should be to two decimal places.

c) Discuss the impact on the selling prices and the sales volumes OF EACH PRODUCT which a change to activity based costing would be expected to bring about.

Solution :

a) Full budgeted production cost per unit using absorption costing

Product	X	Y	Z	Total
Budgeted annual production (units)	20,000	16,000	22,000	
Labour hours per unit	2.5	3	2	
Total labour hours	**50,000**	**48,000**	**44,000**	**1,42,000**

Overhead absorption rate = Rs.1,377,400/142,000=Rs.9·70 per hour

Product	X	Y	Z
	Rs per unit	Rs per unit	Rs per unit
Direct materials	25	28	22
Direct labour	30	36	24
Overhead (Rs 9.70 x 2.5/3/2)	24.25	29.10	19.40
Full Cost per unit	**79.25**	**93.10**	**65.40**

b) Full budgeted production cost per unit using activity based costing

Products	X	Y	Z	Total
Budgeted annual production (units)	20,000	16,000	22,000	
Batch size	500	800	400	
Number of batches (i.e. set ups)	40	20	55	115
Number of purchase orders per batch	4	5	4	
Total Number of orders	160	100	220	480
Machine hours per unit	1.5	1.25	1.4	
Total machine hours	30,000	20,000	30,800	80,800

Cost driver rates:

Cost per Machine set up	Rs. 280.000/115 = Rs. 2.434.78
Cost per order	Rs. 316.000/480 = Rs. 658.33
Cost per Machine hour	(Rs. 420,000 + Rs. 361,400)/80,800 = Rs. 9.67

Allocation of overheads to each product:

Product	X RS	Y RS	Z RS	Total
Machine set up costs	97,391	48,696	133,919	280,000
Material ordering costs	105,333	65,833	144,834	316,000
Machine running and facility costs	290,100	193,400	297,836	781,336*
Total	492,824	307,929	576,583	1,377,336
Number of units produced	20,000	16,000	22,000	
Overhead cost per unit	Rs 24.64	Rs 19.25	Rs 26.21	
Total cost per unit:	**Rs per unit**	**Rs per unit**	**Rs per unit**	
Direct materials	25	28	22	
Direct labour	30	36	44	
Overhead	24.64	19.25	26.21	
ABC cost per unit	79.64	83.25	72.21	

*A difference of Rs64 arises here as compared to the cost pool total of Rs781,400 because of rounding differences. This has been ignored.

c) When activity based costing is used, the cost for product X is very similar to that cost calculated using full absorption costing .This means that the price for product X is likely to remain unchanged because cost plus pricing is being used. Demand for product X is relatively elastic but since no change in price is expected, sales volumes are likely to remain the same if ABC is introduced.

However, the cost for product Y is almost Rs.10 per unit less using ABC. This means that the price of product Y will go down if cost plus pricing is used. Given that demand for product Y is also elastic, like demand for product X, a reduced selling price is likely to give rise to increased sales volumes.

The cost of product Z is nearly Rs.7 per unit more using ABC and the price of product Z will there fore goup if ABC is used. Given that demand for product Z is relatively inelastic, this means that sales volumes would be expected to be largely unchanged despite an increase in price.

Problem 6 :

Maharashtra Limited has collected the following data for its two activities.it calculates activity cost rates based on cost driver capacity.

Activity	Cost Driver	Capacity	Cost
Power	Kilowatt hours	50,000 kilowatt hours	Rs. 2,00,000
Quality Inspections	Number of Inspections	10,000 Inspections	Rs. 3,00,000

The company makes three products M, S and T. For the year ended March 31,2023, the following consumption of cost drivers was reported:

Product	Kilowatt hours	Quality Inspections
M	10,000	3,500
S	20,000	2,500
T	15,000	3,500

Required:

i. COMPUTE the costs allocated to each product from each activity.

ii. CALCULATE the cost of unused capacity for each activity.

iii. DISCUSS the factors the management considers in capacity level to compute the budgeted fixed overhead cost rate.

Solution :

i. Statement of cost allocation to each product from each activity

	Product			
	M (Rs)	**S (Rs)**	**T (Rs)**	**Total (Rs)**
Power (Refer To working Note)	40,000 (10,000 kWh X Rs. 4)	80,000 (20,000 kWh X Rs. 4)	60,000 (15,000 kWh X Rs. 4)	1,80,000
Quality Inspections (Refer to working note)	1,05,000 (3,500 inspections x Rs. 30)	75 ,000 (2,500 inspections x Rs. 30)	90,000 (3,000 inspections x Rs. 30)	2,70,000

Working note :

Rate per unit of cost driver :

Power	(Rs.2,00,000 / 50,000 kWh)	Rs.4/kWh
Quality Inspections	(Rs.3,00,000 / 10,000 inspections)	Rs.30 per inspection

ii. Computation of cost of unused capacity for each activity:

	(Rs)
Power (Rs. 2,00,000-Rs. 1,80,000)	20,000
Quality Inspections (Rs. 3,00,000 - Rs. 2,70,000)	30,000
Total cost of unused capacity	50,000

iii. Factors management consider in choosing a capacity level to compute the budgeted fixed overhead cost rate:

- Effect on product costing & capacity management
- Effect on pricing decisions.
- Effect on performance evaluation
- Effect on financial statements
- Regulatory requirements.
- Difficulties in forecasting chosen capacity level concepts.

❁❁❁❁❁❁

Exercise

Problem 1 :

PQR Ltd. Manufactures two types of machinery Y and Z and Applies/absorbs overheads on the basis of direct-labour hours. The budgeted Overheads and direct-labour hours for month of December, 2019 are Rs 12,42,500 and 20,000 hours respectively. The information about Company's Products is as follows:

	Equipment Y	Equipment Z
Budgeted production volume	2,500 units	3,125 units
Direct material cost	Rs. 300 per unit	Rs. 450 per unit
Direct labour cost Y :3 hours @Rs 150 per hour Z :4 hours @Rs 150 per hour	Rs. 450	Rs. 600

PQR Ltd.'s overheads of Rs. 12,42,500 can be identified with three major activities: Order processing (Rs.2,10,000), machine processing (Rs. 8,75,000), and product inspection (Rs. 1,57,500). These activites are driven by number of orders processed, machine hours worked, and inspection hours worked, and inspection hours, respectively. The data relevant to these activities is as follows:

	Orders processed	Machine hours worked	Inspection hours
Y	350	23,000	4,000
Z	250	27,000	11,000
Total	**600**	**50,000**	**15,000**

Required:

i. Assuming use of direct-labour hours to absorb/apply overheads to production, COMPUTE the unit manufacturing cost of the equipment Y and Z, if the budgeted manufacturing volume is attained.

ii. Assuming use of activity-based costing, COMPUTE the unit manufacturing costs of the equipment Y and Z, if the budgeted manufacturing volume is achieved.

iii. PQR Ltd.'s selling price are based heavily on cost. By using direct-labour hours as an application base, CALCULATE the amount of cost distortion (under-costed or over-costed) for each equipment.

❁❁❁❁❁❁

Multiple Choice Questions

1) **The hierarchy which is based on different types of cost allocation and drivers to categorize cost pool activity is classified as --------------.**
   a) cost hierarchy b) price hierarchy
   c) activity hierarchy d) purpose hierarchy

2) **Assigning overhead using ABC often --------------.**
   a) Shifts overhead costs from high-volume products to low-volume products
   b) Shifts overhead costs from low-volume products to high-volume products
   c) Provides the same results as traditional costing
   d) Requires one predetermined overhead rate

3) **Painting the product would be an example of which activity level groups ------------.**
   a) Facility-level activity b) Product-level activity
   c) Unit-level activity d) Batch-level activity

4) **In an activity based cost system; an activity/ unit of work or task with differentiated purposes will be classified as --------------.**
   a) different task b) purpose cost
   c) an activity d) an allocation cost

5) **In an activity based costing implementation, the product's diverse demand is based on --------------.**
   a) batch size b) complexity c) process steps d) all of above

6) **In the activity based costing method implementation, the indirect costs are allocated by using the --------------.**
   a) no cost pool b) One or two cost pools
   c) sustained tracing d) support tracing

7) **In activity based cost system, the activity, unit of work or task with dillerentiated purpose is classified as --------------.**
   a) different task b) purpose cost c) activity d) allocation cost

8) **In the activity based costing implementation. the pr0duct's diverse demand is based on --------------.**
   a) batch size b) complexity c) process steps d) All of Above

9) **In activity based costing system, the description of activity is classified as --------------.**
   a) activity list b) activity dictionary
   c) active purpose d) both a and b

10) The costing system in which individual activities are identified as the cost object is considered as --------------.

a) manufactured costing
b) activity based costing
c) allocation costing
d) base costing

11) In the activity based costing method implementation, the output unit level costs are classified as --------------.

a) indirect costs
b) direct cost
c) labor cost
d) raw material cost

12) Which of the following is least likely to be classified as a facility-level activity in an activity-based costing system?

a) Plant maintenance
b) Property taxes
c) Machine processing cost
d) Plant depreciation

13) Activity-based costing systems --------------.

a) Use a single, volume-based cost driver.
b) Assign overhead to products based on the products' relative usage of direct labor.
c) Often reveal products that were under- or over-costed by traditional costing systems.
d) typically use fewer cost drivers than more traditional costing systems

14) If the following organizations, activity-based costing cannot be used by --------------.

a) Manufacturers.
b) Financial-services firms.
c) Book publishers.
d) None of the above, as all is able to use this costing system.

15) Activity Based Costing is developed by --------------.

a) Kaplan & Cooper
b) Ouchy
c) Taichi Okno
d) Moulin

16) -------------- is a technique of costing which is based on the benefit received from indirect costs.

a) Life Cycle costing
b) Target costing
c) Activity based costing
a) Standard costing

17) In Activity based costing, the cost of an activity in called --------------.

b) Cost driver
c) Target cost
d) Cost pool
e) Cost object.

18) In activity based costing, -------------- are the factors which influences the cost.

a) Cost pool
b) Cost centre
c) Cost driver
d) Cost object

19) In Activity based Costing, a factor which causes cost is usually called as--------------.

a) Cost driver
b) Governing factor
c) Key factor
d) Limiting factor

20) The costs of underta%en activities to support individual products are classified as --------------.

a) expected sustaining
b) input sustaining
c) output sustaining
d) product sustaining costs

Ans : **1)** a, **2)** a, **3)** c, **4)** c, **5)** d, **6)** b, **7)** c, **8)** d, **9)** d, **10)** b, **11)** a, **12)** c, **13)** d, **14)** d, **15)** a, **16)** c, **17)** c, **18)** c, **19)** a, **20)** d.

❀❀❀❀❀❀

Review Questions

Q. 1. What is Activity Based Costing ? Explain the Scope of Activity Based Costing.

Q. 2. Explain the Nature of Activity Based Costing.

Q. 3. What is Cost Driver ? Explain the Types and Example of Cost Driver.

Q. 4. What are the steps involved in Activity Based Costing ?

Q. 4. Explain the Steps for Calculating Activity Based Costing for a Product.

Q. 5. Explain the Advantages & Disadvantages of Activity Based Costing.

Q. 5. Write a short note on following :

a) Cost Pools.

b) Distinction between Traditional Product Costing and ABC.

c) Main Activity and its Cost Drivers.

d) Scope of Activity Based Costing

e) Activity.

f) Advantages of Activity Based Costing.

❀❀❀❀❀❀